W9-CAB-774

Bloom's
GUIDES

Franz Kafka's
The Metamorphosis

The Adventures of Huckleberry Finn
All the Pretty Horses
Animal Farm
Beloved
Brave New World
The Catcher in the Rye
The Chosen
The Crucible
Cry, the Beloved Country
Death of a Salesman
Fahrenheit 451
The Glass Menagerie
The Grapes of Wrath
Great Expectations
The Great Gatsby
Hamlet
The Handmaid's Tale
The House on Mango Street
I Know Why the Caged Bird Sings
The Iliad
Lord of the Flies
Macbeth
Maggie: A Girl of the Streets
The Member of the Wedding
The Metamorphosis
Of Mice and Men
1984
The Odyssey
One Hundred Years of Solitude
Pride and Prejudice
Ragtime
Romeo and Juliet
Slaughterhouse-Five
The Scarlet Letter
Snow Falling on Cedars
A Streetcar Named Desire
A Tale of Two Cities
The Things They Carried
To Kill a Mockingbird

Bloom's
GUIDES

Franz Kafka's
The Metamorphosis

Edited & with an Introduction
by Harold Bloom

CHELSEA HOUSE
PUBLISHERS
An imprint of Infobase Publishing

Bloom's Guides: The Metamorphosis

Copyright ©2007 by Infobase Publishing
Introduction ©2007 by Harold Bloom

All rights reserved. No part of this book may be reproduced or utilized in any form or by any means, electronic or mechanical, including photocopying, recording, or by any information storage or retrieval systems, without permission in writing from the publisher. For information contact:

Chelsea House
An imprint of Infobase Publishing
132 West 31st Street
New York NY 10001

Library of Congress Cataloging-in-Publication Data
Franz Kafka's The metamorphosis / Harold Bloom, editor.
  p. cm. — (Bloom's guides)
  Includes bibliographical references and index.
  ISBN 0-7910-9298-4 (hardcover)
  1. Kafka, Franz, 1883–1924. Verwandlung. I. Bloom, Harold.
PT2621.A26V282 2007
833'.912—dc22   2006025342

Chelsea House books are available at special discounts when purchased in bulk quantities for businesses, associations, institutions, or sales promotions. Please call our Special Sales Department in New York at (212) 967-8800 or (800) 322-8755.

You can find Chelsea House on the World Wide Web at
http://www.chelseahouse.com

Contributing Editor: Aaron Tillman
Cover design by Takeshi Takahashi

Printed in the United States of America

Bang EJB 10 9 8 7 6 5 4 3 2 1

This book is printed on acid-free paper.

All links and web addresses were checked and verified to be correct at the time of publication. Because of the dynamic nature of the web, some addresses and links may have changed since publication and may no longer be valid.

Contents

 Introduction

HAROLD BLOOM

In her obituary for her lover, Franz Kafka, Milena Jesenská sketched a modern Gnostic, a writer whose vision was of the *kenoma*, the cosmic emptiness into which we have been thrown:

> He was a hermit, a man of insight who was frightened by life.... He saw the world as being full of invisible demons which assail and destroy defenseless man.... All his works describe the terror of mysterious misconceptions and guiltless guilt in human beings.

Milena—brilliant, fearless, and loving—may have subtly distorted Kafka's beautifully evasive slidings between normative Jewish and Jewish Gnostic stances. Max Brod, responding to Kafka's now-famous remark—"We are nihilistic thoughts that came into God's head"—explained to his friend the Gnostic notion that the Demiurge had made this world both sinful and evil. "No," Kafka replied, "I believe we are not such a radical relapse of God's, only one of His bad moods. He had a bad day." Playing straight man, the faithful Brod asked if this meant there was hope outside our cosmos. Kafka smiled, and charmingly said: "Plenty of hope—for God—no end of hope— only not for us."

Kafka, despite Gershom Scholem's authoritative attempts to claim him for Jewish Gnosticism, is both more and less than a Gnostic, as we might expect. Yahweh can be saved, and the divine degradation that is fundamental to Gnosticism is not an element in Kafka's world. But we were fashioned out of the clay during one of Yahweh's bad moods; perhaps there was divine dyspepsia, or sultry weather in the garden that Yahweh had planted in the East. Yahweh is hope, and we are hopeless. We are the jackdaws or crows, the kafkas (since that is what the name means, in Czech) whose impossibility is what the heavens signify: "The crows maintain that a single crow could destroy the heavens. Doubtless that is so, but it proves nothing against the heavens, for the heavens signify simply: the impossibility of crows."

In Gnosticism, there is an alien, wholly transcendent God, and the adept, after considerable difficulties, can find the way back to presence and fullness. Gnosticism therefore is a religion of salvation, though the most negative of all such saving visions. Kafkan spirituality offers no hope of salvation, and so is not Gnostic. But Milena Jesenská certainly was right to emphasize the Kafkan terror that is akin to Gnosticism's dread of the *kenoma*, which is the world governed by the Archons. Kafka takes the impossible step beyond Gnosticism, by denying that there is hope for us anywhere at all.

In the aphorisms that Brod rather misleadingly entitled "Reflections on Sin, Pain, Hope and The True Way," Kafka wrote: "What is laid upon us is to accomplish the negative; the positive is already given." How much Kabbalah Kafka knew is not clear. Since he wrote a new Kabbalah, the question of Jewish Gnostic sources can be set aside. Indeed, by what seems a charming oddity (but I would call it yet another instance of Blake's insistence that forms of worship are chosen from poetic tales), our understanding of Kabbalah is Kafkan anyway, since Kafka profoundly influenced Gershom Scholem, and no one will be able to get beyond Scholem's creative or strong misreading of Kabbalah for decades to come. I repeat this point to emphasize its shock value: we read Kabbalah, via Scholem, from a Kafkan perspective, even as we read human personality and its mimetic possibilities by way of Shakespeare's perspectives, since essentially Freud mediates Shakespeare for us, yet relies upon him nevertheless. A Kafkan facticity or contingency now governs our awareness of whatever in Jewish cultural tradition is other than normative.

In his diaries for 1922, Kafka meditated, on January 16, upon "something very like a breakdown," in which it was "impossible to sleep, impossible to stay awake, impossible to endure life, or, more exactly, the course of life." The vessels were breaking for him as his demoniac, writerly inner world and the outer life "split apart, and they do split apart, or at least clash in a fearful manner." Late in the evening, K. arrives at the village, which is deep in snow. The Castle is in front of him, but even the hill upon which it stands is veiled in mist and darkness, and there is not a single light visible to show that the Castle was there. K. stands a long time on a wooden bridge that leads from the main road to the village, while gazing, not at the village, but "into the illusory emptiness above him," where the Castle should be. He does not know what he will always refuse to learn, which is that the emptiness is "illusory" in every possible sense, since he does gaze at the *kenoma*, which resulted initially from the breaking of the vessels, the splitting apart of every world, inner and outer.

Writing the vision of K., Kafka counts the costs of his confirmation, in a passage prophetic of Scholem, but with a difference that Scholem sought to negate by combining Zionism and Kabbalah for himself. Kafka knew better, perhaps only for himself, but perhaps for others as well:

Second: This pursuit, originating in the midst of men, carries one in a direction away from them. The solitude that for the most part has been forced on me, in part voluntarily sought by me—but what was this if not compulsion too?—is now losing all its ambiguity and approaches its denouement. Where is it leading? The strongest likelihood is that it may lead to madness; there is nothing more to say, the pursuit goes right through me and rends me asunder. Or I can—can I?—manage to keep my feet somewhat and be carried along in the wild pursuit. Where, then, shall I be brought? "Pursuit," indeed, is only a metaphor. I can also say, "assault on the last earthly frontier," an assault, moreover, launched from below, from mankind, and since this too is a metaphor, I can replace it by the metaphor of an assault from above, aimed at me from above.

All such writing is an assault on the frontiers; if Zionism had not intervened, it might easily have developed into a new secret doctrine, a Kabbalah. There are intimations of this. Though of course it would require genius of an unimaginable kind to strike root again in the old centuries, or create the old centuries anew and not spend itself withal, but only then begin to flower forth.

Consider Kafka's three metaphors, which he so knowingly substitutes for one another. The pursuit is of ideas, in that mode of introspection which is Kafka's writing. Yet this metaphor of pursuit is also a piercing "right through me" and a breaking apart of the self. For "pursuit," Kafka then substitutes mankind's assault, from below, on the last earthly frontier. What is that frontier? It must lie between us and the heavens. Kafka, the crow or jackdaw, by writing, transgresses the frontier and implicitly maintains that he could destroy the heavens. By another substitution, the metaphor changes to "an assault from above, aimed at me from above," the aim simply being the signifying function of the heavens, which is to mean the impossibility of Kafkas or crows. The heavens assault Kafka *through his writing*; "all such writing is an assault on the frontiers," and these must now be Kafka's own frontiers. One thinks of Freud's most complex "frontier concept," more complex even than the drive: the bodily ego. The heavens assault Kafka's bodily ego, *but only through his own writing*. Certainly such an assault is not un-Jewish, and has as much to do with normative as with esoteric Jewish tradition.

Yet, according to Kafka, his own writing, were it not for the intervention of Zionism, might easily have developed into a new Kabbalah. How are we to understand that curious statement about Zionism as the blocking agent that prevents Franz Kafka from becoming another Isaac Luria? Kafka darkly and immodestly writes: "There are intimations of this." Our teacher Gershom Scholem governs our interpretation here, of necessity. Those intimations belong to Kafka alone, or perhaps to a select few in his immediate circle. They cannot be conveyed to Jewry, even to its elite, because Zionism has taken the place of messianic Kabbalah, including presumably the heretical Kabbalah of Nathan of Gaza, prophet of Sabbatai Zvi and of all his followers down to the blasphemous Jacob Frank.

Kafka's influence upon Scholem is decisive here, for Kafka already has arrived at Scholem's central thesis of the link between the Kabbalah of Isaac Luria, the messianism of the Sabbatarians and Frankists, and the political Zionism that gave rebirth to Israel.

Kafka goes on, most remarkably, to disown the idea that he possesses "genius of an unimaginable kind," one that either would strike root again in archaic Judaism, presumably of the esoteric sort, or more astonishingly "create the old centuries anew," which Scholem insisted Kafka had done. But can we speak, as Scholem tried to speak, of the Kabbalah of Franz Kafka? Is there a new secret doctrine in the superb stories and the extraordinary parables and paradoxes, or did not Kafka spend his genius in the act of new creation of the old Jewish centuries? Kafka certainly would have judged himself harshly as one spent withal, rather than as a writer who "only then began to flower forth." Kafka died only two and a half years after this meditative moment, died, alas, just before his forty-first birthday. Yet as the propounder of a new Kabbalah, he had gone very probably as far as he (or anyone else) could go. No Kabbalah, be it that of Moses de Leon, Isaac Luria, Moses Cordovero, Nathan of Gaza or Gershom Scholem, is exactly easy to interpret, but Kafka's secret doctrine, if it exists at all, is designedly uninterpretable. My working principle in reading Kafka is to observe that he did everything possible to evade interpretation, which only means that what most needs and demands interpretation in Kafka's writing is its perversely deliberate evasion of interpretation. Erich Heller's formula for getting at this evasion is: "Ambiguity has never been considered an elemental force; it is precisely this in the stories of Franz Kafka." Perhaps, but evasiveness is not the same literary quality as ambiguity.

Evasiveness is purposive; it writes between the lines, to borrow a fine trope from Leo Strauss. What does it mean when a quester for a new Negative, or perhaps rather a revisionist of an old Negative, resorts to the evasion of every possible interpretation as his central topic or theme? Kafka does not doubt guilt, but wishes to make it "possible for men to enjoy sin without guilt, almost without guilt," by reading Kafka. To enjoy sin almost without guilt is to evade interpretation, in exactly the dominant Jewish sense of interpretation. Jewish tradition, whether normative or esoteric, never teaches you to ask Nietzsche's question: "Who is the interpreter, and what power does he seek to gain over the text?" Instead, Jewish tradition asks: "Is the interpreter in the line of those who seek to build a hedge about the Torah in every age?" Kafka's power of evasiveness is not a power over his own text, and it does build a hedge about the Torah in our age. Yet no one before Kafka built up that hedge wholly out of evasiveness, not even Maimonides or Judah Halevi or even Spinoza. Subtlest and most evasive of all writers, Kafka remains the severest and most harassing of the belated sages of what will yet become the Jewish cultural tradition of the future.

II

The jackdaw or crow or Kafka is also the weird figure of the great hunter Gracchus (whose Latin name also means a crow), who is not alive but dead, yet who floats, like one living, on his death-bark forever. When the fussy Burgomaster of Riva knits his brow, asking: "And you have no part in the other world (*das Jenseits*)?", the Hunter replies, with grand defensive irony:

> I am forever on the great stair that leads up to it. On that infinitely wide and spacious stair I clamber about, sometimes up, sometimes down, sometimes on the right, sometimes on the left, always in motion. The Hunter has been turned into a butterfly. Do not laugh.

Like the Burgomaster, we do not laugh. Being a single crow, Gracchus would be enough to destroy the heavens, but he will never get there. Instead, the heavens signify his impossibility, the absence of crows or hunters, and so he has been turned into another butterfly, which is all we can be, from the perspective of the heavens. And we bear no blame for that:

"I had been glad to live and I was glad to die. Before I stepped aboard, I joyfully flung away my wretched load of ammunition, my knapsack, my hunting rifle that I had always been proud to carry, and I slipped into my winding sheet like a girl into her marriage dress. I lay and waited. Then came the mishap."

"A terrible fate," said the Burgomaster, raising his hand defensively. "And you bear no blame for it?"

"None," said the hunter. "I was a hunter; was there any sin in that? I followed my calling as a hunter in the Black Forest, where there were still wolves in those days. I lay in ambush, shot, hit my mark, flayed the skin from my victims: was there any sin in that? My labors were blessed. 'The Great Hunter of Black Forest' was the name I was given. Was there any sin in that?"

"I am not called upon to decide that," said the Burgomaster, "but to me also there seems to be no sin in such things. But then, whose is the guilt?"

"The boatman's," said the Hunter. "Nobody will read what I say here, no one will come to help me; even if all the people were commanded to help me, every door and window would remain shut, everybody would take to bed and draw the bedclothes over his head, the whole earth would become an inn for the night. And there is sense in that, for nobody knows of me, and if anyone knew he would not know where I could be found, and if he knew where I could be found, he would not know how to deal with me, he would not know how to help me. The thought of helping me is an illness that has to be cured by taking to one's bed."

How admirable Gracchus is, even when compared to the Homeric heroes! They know, or think they know, that to be alive, however miserable, is preferable to being the foremost among the dead. But Gracchus wished only to be himself, happy to be a hunter when alive, joyful to be a corpse when dead: "I slipped into my winding sheet like a girl into her marriage dress." So long as everything happened in good order, Gracchus was more than content. The guilt must be the boatman's, and may not exceed mere incompetence. Being dead and yet still articulate, Gracchus is beyond help: "The thought of helping me is an illness that has to be cured by taking to one's bed."

When he gives the striking trope of the whole earth closing down like an inn for the night, with the bedclothes drawn over everybody's head, Gracchus renders the judgment: "And there is sense in that." There is sense in that only because in Kafka's world as in Freud's, or in Scholem's, or in any world deeply informed by Jewish memory, there is necessarily sense in everything, total sense, even though Kafka refuses to aid you in getting at or close to it.

But what kind of a world is that, where there is sense in everything, where everything seems to demand interpretation? There can be sense in everything, as J. H. Van den Berg once wrote against Freud's theory of repression, only if everything is already in the past and there never again can be anything wholly new. That is certainly the world of the great normative rabbis of the second century of the Common Era, and consequently it has been the world of most Jews ever since. Torah has been given, Talmud has risen to complement and interpret it, other interpretations in the chain of tradition are freshly forged in each generation, but the limits of Creation and of Revelation are fixed in Jewish memory. There is sense in everything because all sense is present already in the Hebrew Bible, which by definition must be totally intelligible, even if its fullest intelligibility will not shine forth until the Messiah comes.

Gracchus, hunter and jackdaw, is Kafka, pursuer of ideas and jackdaw, and the endless, hopeless voyage of Gracchus is Kafka's passage, only partly through a language not his own, and largely through a life not much his own. Kafka was studying Hebrew intensively while he wrote "The Hunter Gracchus," early in 1917, and I think we may call the voyages of the dead but never-buried Gracchus a trope for Kafka's belated study of his ancestral language. He was still studying

Hebrew in the spring of 1923, with his tuberculosis well advanced, and down to nearly the end he longed for Zion, dreaming of recovering his health and firmly grounding his identity by journeying to Palestine. Like Gracchus, he experienced life-in-death, though unlike Gracchus he achieved the release of total death.

"The Hunter Gracchus" as a story or extended parable is not the narrative of a Wandering Jew or Flying Dutchman, because Kafka's trope for his writing activity is not so much a wandering or even a wavering, but rather a repetition, labyrinthine and burrow-building. His writing repeats, not itself, but a Jewish esoteric interpretation of Torah that Kafka himself scarcely knows, or even needs to know. What this interpretation tells Kafka is that there is no written Torah but only an oral one. However, Kafka has no one to tell him what this Oral Torah is. He substitutes his own writing therefore for the Oral Torah not made available to him. He is precisely in the stance of the Hunter Gracchus, who concludes by saying, "'I am here, more than that I do not know, further than that I cannot go. My ship has no rudder, and it is driven by the wind that blows in the undermost regions of death.'"

III

"What is the Talmud if not a message from the distance?", Kafka wrote to Robert Klopstock, on December 19, 1932. What was all of Jewish tradition, to Kafka, except a message from an endless distance? That is surely part of the burden of the famous parable, "An Imperial Message," which concludes with you, the reader, sitting at your window when evening falls and dreaming to yourself the parable—that God, in his act of dying, has sent you an individual message. Heinz Politzer read this as a Nietzschean parable, and so fell into the trap set by the Kafkan evasiveness:

Describing the fate of the parable in a time depleted of metaphysical truths, the imperial message has turned into the subjective fantasy of a dreamer who sits at a window with a view on a darkening world. The only real information imported by this story is the news of the Emperor's death. This news Kafka took over from Nietzsche.

No, for even though you dream the parable, the parable conveys truth. The Talmud does exist; it really is an Imperial message from the distance. The distance is too great; it cannot reach you; there is hope, but not for you. Nor is it so clear that God is dead. He is always dying, yet always whispers a message into the angel's ear. It is said to you that: "Nobody could fight his way through here even with a message from a dead man," but the Emperor actually does not die in the text of the parable.

Distance is part of Kafka's crucial notion of the Negative, which is not a Hegelian nor a Heideggerian Negative, but is very close to Freud's Negation and also to the Negative imaging carried out by Scholem's Kabbalists. But I want to postpone Kafka's Jewish version of the Negative until later. "The Hunter Gracchus" is an extraordinary text, but it is not wholly characteristic of Kafka at his strongest, at his uncanniest or most sublime.

When he is most himself, Kafka gives us a continuous inventiveness and originality that rivals Dante, and truly challenges Proust and Joyce as that of the dominant Western author of our century, setting Freud aside, since Freud ostensibly is science and not narrative or mythmaking, though if you believe that, then you can be persuaded of anything. Kafka's beast fables are rightly celebrated, but his most remarkable fabulistic being is neither animal nor human, but is little Odradek, in the curious sketch, less than a page and a half long, "The Cares of a Family Man," where the title might have been translated: "The Sorrows of a Paterfamilias." The family man narrates these five paragraphs, each a dialectical lyric in itself, beginning with one that worries the meaning of the name:

Some say the word Odradek is of Slavonic origin, and try to account for it on that basis. Others again believe it to be of German origin, only influenced by Slavonic. The uncertainty of both interpretations allows one to assume with justice that neither is accurate, especially as neither of them provides an intelligent meaning of the word.

This evasiveness was overcome by the scholar Wilhelm Emrich, who traced the name Odradek to the Czech word *odraditi*, meaning to dissuade anyone from doing anything. Like Edward Gorey's Doubtful Guest, Odradek is uninvited yet will not leave, since implicitly he dissuades you from doing anything about his presence, or rather something about his very uncanniness advises you to let him alone:

> No one, of course, would occupy himself with such studies if there were not a creature called Odradek. At first glance it looks like a flat star-shaped spool for thread, and indeed it does seem to have thread wound upon it; to be sure, they are only old, broken-off bits of thread, knotted and tangled together, of the most varied sorts and colors. But it is not only a spool, for a small wooden crossbar sticks out of the middle of the star, and another small rod is joined to that at a right angle. By means of this latter rod on one side and one of the points of the star on the other, the whole thing can stand upright as if on two legs.

Is Odradek a "thing," as the bemused family man begins by calling him, or is he not a childlike creature, a daemon at home in the world of children? Odradek clearly was made by an inventive and humorous child, rather in the spirit of the making of Adam out of the moistened red clay by the J writer's Yahweh. It is difficult not to read Odradek's creation as a deliberate parody when we are told that "the whole thing can stand upright as if on two legs," and again when the suggestion is ventured that Odradek, like Adam, "once had some sort of intelligible shape and is now only a broken-down remnant." If Odradek is fallen, he is still quite jaunty, and cannot be closely scrutinized, since he "is extraordinarily nimble and can never be laid hold of," like the story in which he appears. Odradek not only advises you not to do anything about him, but in some clear sense he is yet another figure by means of whom Kafka advises you against interpreting Kafka.

One of the loveliest moments in all of Kafka comes when you, the *paterfamilias*, encounter Odradek leaning directly beneath you against the banisters. Being inclined to speak to him, as you would to a child, you receive a surprise: "'Well, what's your name?' you ask him. 'Odradek,' he says. 'And where do you live?' 'No fixed abode,' he says and laughs; but it is only the kind of laughter that has no lungs behind it. It sounds rather like the rustling of fallen leaves."

"The 'I' is another," Rimbaud once wrote, adding: "So much the worse for the wood that finds it is a violin." So much the worse for the wood that finds it is Odradek. He laughs at being a vagrant, if only by the bourgeois definition of having "no fixed abode," but the laughter, not being human, is uncanny. And so he provokes the family man to an uncanny reflection, which may be a Kafkan parody of Freud's death drive beyond the pleasure principle:

I ask myself, to no purpose, what is likely to happen to him? Can he possibly die? Anything that dies has had some kind of aim in life, some kind of activity, which has worn out; but that does not apply to Odradek. Am I to suppose, then, that he will always be rolling down the stairs, with ends of thread trailing after him, right before the feet of my children? He does no harm to anyone that I can see, but the idea that he is likely to survive me I find almost painful.

The aim of life, Freud says, is death, is the return of the organic to the inorganic, supposedly our earlier state of being. Our activity wears out, and so we die because, in an uncanny sense, we wish to die. But Odradek, harmless and charming, is a child's creation, aimless, and so not subject to the death drive. Odradek is immortal, being daemonic, and he represents also a Freudian return of the repressed, of something repressed in the *paterfamilias*, something from which the family man is in perpetual flight. Little Odradek is precisely what Freud calls a cognitive return of the repressed, while (even as) a complete affective repression is maintained. The family man introjects Odradek intellectually, but totally projects him affectively. Odradek, I now suggest, is best understood as Kafka's synecdoche for *Verneinung*; Kafka's version (not altogether un-Freudian) of Jewish Negation, a version I hope to adumbrate in what follows.

IV

Why does Kafka have so unique a spiritual authority? Perhaps the question should be rephrased. What kind of spiritual authority does Kafka have for us or why are we moved or compelled to read him as one who has such authority? Why invoke the question of authority at all? Literary authority, however we define it, has no necessary relation to spiritual authority, and to speak of a spiritual authority in Jewish writing anyway always has been to speak rather dubiously. Authority is not a Jewish concept but a Roman one, and so makes perfect contemporary sense in the context of the Roman Catholic Church, but little sense in Jewish matters, despite the squalors of Israeli politics and the flaccid pieties of American Jewish nostalgias. There is no authority without hierarchy, and hierarchy is not a very Jewish concept either. We do not want the rabbis, or anyone else, to tell us what or who is or is not Jewish. The masks of the normative conceal not only the eclecticism of Judaism and of Jewish culture, but also the nature of the J writer's Yahweh himself. It is absurd to think of Yahweh as having mere authority. He is no Roman godling who augments human activities, nor a Homeric god helping to constitute an audience for human heroism.

Yahweh is neither a founder nor an onlooker, though sometimes he can be mistaken for either or both. His essential trope is fatherhood rather than foundation, and his interventions are those of a covenanter rather than of a spectator. You cannot found an authority upon him, because his benignity is manifested not through augmentation but through creation. He does not write; he speaks, and he is heard, in time, and what he continues to create by his speaking is *olam*, time without boundaries, which is more than just an augmentation. More of anything else can come through authority, but more life is the blessing itself, and comes, beyond authority, to Abraham, to Jacob, and to David. No more than Yahweh, do any of them have mere authority. Yet Kafka certainly does have literary authority, and in a troubled way his literary authority is now spiritual also, particularly in Jewish contexts. I do not think that this is a post-Holocaust phenomenon, though Jewish Gnosticism, oxymoronic as it may or may not be, certainly seems appropriate to our time, to many among us. Literary Gnosticism does not seem to me a time-bound phenomenon, anyway. Kafka's *The Castle*, as Erich Heller has argued, is clearly more Gnostic than normative in is spiritual temper, but then so is Shakespeare's *Macbeth*, and Blake's *The Four Zoas*, and Carlyle's *Sartor Resartus*. We sense a Jewish element in Kafka's apparent Gnosticism, even if we are less prepared than Scholem was to name it as a new Kabbalah. In his 1922 Diaries, Kafka subtly insinuated that even his espousal of the Negative was dialectical:

The Negative alone, however strong it may be, cannot suffice, as in my unhappiest moments I believe it can. For if I have gone the tiniest step upward, won any, be it the most dubious kind of security for myself, I then stretch out on my step and wait for the Negative, not to climb up to me, indeed, but to drag me down from it. Hence it is a defensive instinct in me that won't tolerate my having the slightest degree of lasting ease and smashes the marriage bed, for example, even before it has been set up.

What is the Kafkan Negative, whether in this passage or elsewhere? Let us begin by dismissing the Gallic notion that there is anything Hegelian about it, any more than there is anything Hegelian about the Freudian *Verneinung*. Kafka's Negative, unlike Freud's, is uneasily and remotely descended from the ancient tradition of negative theology, and perhaps even from that most negative of ancient theologies, Gnosticism, and yet Kafka, despite his yearnings for transcendence, joins Freud in accepting the ultimate authority of the fact. The given suffers no destruction in Kafka or in Freud, and this given essentially is the way things are, for everyone, and for the Jews in particular. If fact is supreme, then the mediation of the Hegelian Negative becomes an absurdity, and no destructive use of such a Negative is possible, which is to say that Heidegger becomes impossible, and Derrida, who is a strong misreading of Heidegger, becomes quite unnecessary.

The Kafkan Negative most simply is his Judaism, which is to say the spiritual form of Kafka's self-conscious Jewishness, as exemplified in that extraordinary aphorism: "What is laid upon us is to accomplish the negative; the positive is already given." The positive here is the Law or normative Judaism; the negative is not so much Kafka's new Kabbalah, as it is that which is still laid upon us: the Judaism of the Negative, of the future as it is always rushing towards us.

His best biographer to date, Ernst Pawel, emphasizes Kafka's consciousness "of his identity as a Jew, not in the religious, but in the national sense." Still, Kafka was not a Zionist, and perhaps he longed not so much for Zion as for a Jewish language, be it Yiddish or Hebrew. He could not see that his astonishing stylistic purity in German was precisely his way of *not* betraying his self-identity as a Jew. In his final phase, Kafka thought of going to Jerusalem, and again intensified his study of Hebrew. Had he lived, he would probably have gone to Zion, perfected a vernacular Hebrew, and given us the bewilderment of Kafkan parables and stories in the language of the J writer and of Judah Halevi.

V

What calls out for interpretation in Kafka is his refusal to be interpreted, his evasiveness even in the realm of his own Negative. Two of his most beautifully enigmatical performances, both late, are the parable, "The Problem of Our

Laws," and the story or testament "Josephine the Singer and the Mouse Folk." Each allows a cognitive return of Jewish cultural memory, while refusing the affective identification that would make either parable or tale specifically Jewish in either historical or contemporary identification. "The Problem of Our Laws" is set as a problem in the parable's first paragraph:

> Our laws are not generally known; they are kept secret by the small group of nobles who rule us. We are convinced that these ancient laws are scrupulously administered; nevertheless it is an extremely painful thing to be ruled by laws that one does not know. I am not thinking of possible discrepancies that may arise in the interpretation of the laws, or of the disadvantages involved when only a few and not the whole people are allowed to have a say in their interpretation. These disadvantages are perhaps of no great importance. For the laws are very ancient; their interpretation has been the work of centuries, and has itself doubtless acquired the status of law; and though there is still a possible freedom of interpretation left, it has now become very restricted. Moreover the nobles have obviously no cause to be influenced in their interpretation by personal interests inimical to us, for the laws were made to the advantage of the nobles from the very beginning, they themselves stand above the laws, and that seems to be why the laws were entrusted exclusively into their hands. Of course, there is wisdom in that—who doubts the wisdom of the ancient laws?—but also hardship for us; probably that is unavoidable.

In Judaism, the Law is precisely what is generally known, proclaimed, and taught by the normative sages. The Kabbalah was secret doctrine, but increasingly was guarded not by the normative rabbis, but by Gnostic sectaries, Sabbatarians, and Frankists, all of them ideologically descended from Nathan of Gaza, Sabbatai Zvi's prophet. Kafka twists askew the relations between normative and esoteric Judaism, again making a synecdochal representation impossible. It is not the rabbis or normative sages who stand above the Torah but the *minim*, the heretics from Elisha ben Abuyah through to Jacob Frank, and in some sense, Gershom Scholem as well. To these Jewish Gnostics, as the parable goes on to insinuate: "The Law is whatever the nobles do." So radical a definition tells us "that the tradition is far from complete," and that a kind of messianic expectation is therefore necessary. This view, so comfortless as far as the present is concerned, is lightened only by the belief that a time will eventually come when the tradition and our research into it will jointly reach their conclusion, and as it were gain a breathing space, when everything will have become clear, the law will belong to the people, and the nobility will vanish.

If the parable at this point were to be translated into early Christian terms, then "the nobility" would be the Pharisees, and "the people" would be the Christian believers. But Kafka moves rapidly to stop such a translation: "This is not maintained in any spirit of hatred against the nobility; not at all, and by no one. We are more inclined to hate ourselves, because we have not yet shown ourselves worthy of being entrusted with the laws."

"We" here cannot be either Christians or Jews. Who then are those who "have not yet shown ourselves worthy of being entrusted with the laws"? They would appear to be the crows or jackdaws again, a Kafka or a Hunter Gracchus, wandering about in a state perhaps vulnerable to self-hatred or self-distrust, waiting for a Torah that will not be revealed. Audaciously, Kafka then concludes with overt paradox:

> Actually one can express the problem only in a sort of paradox: Any party that would repudiate not only all belief in the laws, but the nobility as well, would have the whole people behind it; yet no such party can come into existence, for nobody would dare to repudiate the nobility. We live on this razor's edge. A writer once summed the matter up in this way: The sole visible and indubitable law that is imposed upon us is the nobility, and must we ourselves deprive ourselves of that one law?

Why would no one dare to repudiate the nobility, whether we read them as normative Pharisees, Jewish Gnostic heresiarchs, or whatever? Though imposed upon us, the sages or the *minim* are the only visible evidence of law that we have. Who are we then? How is the parable's final question, whether open or rhetorical, to be answered? "Must we ourselves deprive ourselves of that one law?" Blake's answer, in *The Marriage of Heaven and Hell*, was: "One Law for the Lion and the Ox is Oppression." But what is one law for the crows? Kafka will not tell us whether it is oppression or not.

Josephine the singer also is a crow or Kafka, rather than a mouse, and the folk may be interpreted as an entire nation of jackdaws. The spirit of the Negative, dominant if uneasy in "The Problem of Our Laws," is loosed into a terrible freedom in Kafka's testamentary story. That is to say: in the parable, the laws could not be Torah, though that analogue flickered near. But in Josephine's story, the mouse folk simultaneously are *and* are not the Jewish people, and Franz Kafka both is *and* is not their curious singer. Cognitively the identifications are possible, as though returned from forgetfulness, but affectively they certainly are not, unless we can assume that crucial aspects making up the identifications have been purposefully, if other than consciously, forgotten. Josephine's piping is Kafka's story, and yet Kafka's story is hardly Josephine's piping.

Can there be a mode of negation neither conscious nor unconscious, neither Hegelian nor Freudian? Kafka's genius provides one, exposing many shades between consciousness and the work of repression, many demarcations far ghostlier than we could have imagined without him. Perhaps the ghostliest come at the end of the story:

> Josephine's road, however, must go downhill. The time will soon come when her last notes sound and die into silence. She is a small episode in the eternal history of our people, and the people will get over the loss of her. Not that it will be easy for us; how can our gatherings take place in utter silence? Still, were they not silent even when Josephine was present? Was her actual piping

notably louder and more alive than the memory of it will be? Was it even in her lifetime more than a simply memory? Was it not rather because Josephine's singing was already past losing in this way that our people in their wisdom prized it so highly?

So perhaps we shall not miss so very much after all, while Josephine, redeemed from the earthly sorrows which to her thinking lay in wait for all chosen spirits, will happily lose herself in the numberless throng of the heroes of our people, and soon, since we are no historians, will rise to the heights of redemption and be forgotten like all her brothers.

"I am a Memory come alive," Kafka wrote in the Diaries. Whether or not he intended it, he was Jewish memory come alive. "Was it even in her lifetime more than a simple memory?" Kafka asks, knowing that he too was past losing. The Jews are no historians, in some sense, because Jewish memory, as Yosef Yerushalmi has demonstrated, is a normative mode and not a historical one. Kafka, if he could have prayed, might have prayed to rise to the heights of redemption and be forgotten like most of his brothers and sisters. But his prayer would not have been answered. When we think of *the* Catholic writer, we think of Dante, who nevertheless had the audacity to enshrine his Beatrice in the hierarchy of Paradise. If we think of *the* Protestant writer, we think of Milton, a party or sect of one, who believed that the soul was mortal, and would be resurrected only in conjunction with the body. Think of *the* Jewish writer, and you must think of Kafka, who evaded his own audacity, and believed nothing, and trusted only in the Covenant of being a writer.

VI

What can it mean to trust in the Covenant, not between Yahweh and the Jewish people, but between writing and a writer? Gregor Samsa is a solitary (his last name, in Czech, can be translated "I am alone"), commercial traveler, and a kind of family pariah or outcast, at least in his own tormented vision. His celebrated metamorphosis, into a kind of huge bedbug, is completed in the story's first sentence. Gregor's fate is certain but without hope; there is plenty of hope, for writing as for God, but none for Gregor. The Law, which is the way things are, including one's parents' huge debt to one's employer, is essentially a universal compulsion to repeat. No irony, however well handled, can represent repetition compulsion as the Law of the Jews. Samsa's employer is therefore not Yahweh, but another version of the Gnostic Demiurge, ruler of the cosmological emptiness in which we dwell.

The only rage to order that Kafka knew was his implicit rage not to be interpreted. There can be no ultimate coherence to my Gnostic interpretation (nor for Scholem's, nor Benjamin's, nor Heller's, nor to anyone's) because Kafka refuses the Gnostic quest for the alien God, for one's own spark or *pneuma* rejoining the original Abyss somewhere out of this world. The huge bedbug is neither the fallen husk of Samsa nor his potentially saving *pneuma*. It can hardly be his spark from the original Abyss because it is a horrible vermin, and yet only after his transformation into a bug is Gregor capable of aesthetic apprehension. Like Shakespeare's grotesque Caliban, the insect Samsa hears the beautiful in music, and so for the first time apprehends another sphere. Kafka refused an illustration for *The Metamorphosis* that would have portrayed Gregor Samsa as a literal beetle or bedbug: "The insect itself cannot be drawn. It cannot be drawn even as if seen from a distance." This is not to say that Samsa suffers an hallucination, but only reminds us that a negation cannot be visually represented, which in turn reminds us of Kafkan nostalgias for the Second Commandment.

Is Gregor accurate in his final consciousness that his death is a liberation, an act of love for his family? Wilhelm Emrich, elsewhere so wary a Kafka exegete, fell into this momentary passion for the positive, an entrapment all readers of Kafka suffer sooner or later, so exhausted are we by this greatest master of evasions. Because the insect is inexplicable, it does not necessarily contain any truth. *The Metamorphosis*, like all crucial Kafkan narratives, takes place somewhere *between* truth and meaning, a "somewhere" identical with the modern Jewish rupture from the normative tradition. Truth is in hope and neither is available to us, while meaning is in the future or the messianic age, and we will not come up to either. We are lazy, but industry will not avail us either, not even the industrious zeal with which every writer prides himself upon accepting his own death. If *the Metamorphosis* is a satire, then it is self-satire, or post-Nietzschean parody, that humiliates Kafka's only covenant, the placing of trust in the transcendental possibility of being a strong writer.

The story then cannot be interpreted coherently as a fantasy of death and resurrection, or as an allegory on the less-is-more fate of being a writer. Gregor's death is not an effectual sacrifice, not a self-fulfillment, and not even a tragic irony of any kind. It is another Kafkan negation that refuses to negate the given, which is the world of Freud's reality principle. Gregor does not become a child again as he dies. Yet we cannot even call him a failure, which might guarantee his upward fall to heights of redemption. Like Gracchus, like the bucket-rider, like the country doctor, like the hunger artist, Gregor is suspended between the truth of the past, or Jewish memory, and the meaning of the future, or Jewish messianism. Poor Gregor therefore evades the categories both of belief and of poetry. How much would most of us know about this rupture without Kafka, or Kafka's true heir, Beckett?

A Gnosticism without transcendence is not a knowing but is something else, and there is no transcendence in the *Metamorphosis*, or anywhere in Kafka. To transcend in a world of rupture you only need to change your direction, but that is to adopt the stance of the cat (or Gnostic archon) of Kafka's magnificent and appalling parable, "A Little Fable":

> "Alas," said the mouse, "the world is growing smaller every day. At the beginning it was so big that I was afraid, I kept running and running, and I was glad when at last I saw walls far away to the right and left, but these long walls have narrowed so quickly that I am in the last

chamber already, and there in the corner stands the trap that I must run into." "You only need to change your direction," said the cat, and ate it up.

(Translated by Willa and Edwin Muir)

Biographical Sketch

Franz Kafka was born in Prague on July 3, 1883, the first child of German-Jewish parents, Hermann and Julie Kafka. Franz's father, Hermann, owned a dry goods store and was portrayed in Kafka's "Letter to my Father" as a strict and largely unsympathetic man. In 1885, Franz's brother Georg was born, but he died the following year. Two years later, another brother Heinrich was born, but he too died within the same year. Finally in September, 1889, around the same time that Franz first entered a German elementary school, the first of his three sisters, Gabriele, was born. The following year, his second sister Valerie was born, and in 1892, his youngest sister Ottilie was born. In 1893, Franz began attending the German Gymnasium of Prague. He had his Bar Mitzvah in 1896 and graduated from his German high school in 1901.

From 1901 to 1906, Kafka studied law at Charles Ferdinand University, a German college in Prague. During his second year, he met Max Brod who would become his closest confidant, eventual biographer, and one of his translators. While in school, Kafka began writing *Description of a Struggle*. In 1906, he graduated with a degree in law and was soon hired as a secretary in a law office.

The year after graduating from college, Kafka wrote "Wedding Preparations in the Country," and by the following year, he had eight pieces of prose published in the literary review *Hyperion*; these pieces would later appear in his first book, *Meditation*. It was during this year, 1908, when Kafka began working with the Workers' Accident Insurance Institute, where he would remain employed for the majority of his life. In 1909, the Prague newspaper *Bohemia*, published "The Aeroplanes at Brescia," and over the course of the next year, they published five more of Kafka's prose pieces, all of which would appear in *Meditation*.

In 1910 and 1911, Kafka traveled to Bohemia, France, Germany, Switzerland and Italy with Max Brod. During his travels, he developed a keen interest in Yiddish theater and literature. 1912 was a fruitful year for Kafka who began work on his first novel, *Amerika*, completed "The Judgment" and "The Metamorphosis," and met Felice Bauer, the woman whom he would get engaged to twice, and to whom hundreds of pages of letters would be written. The following year, his book *Meditation* was finally published, as was "The Judgment" and "The Stoker," which later became the first chapter in his novel *Amerika*.

Kafka first became engaged to Felice Bauer in 1914, but later that year he broke it off. During this time, he wrote "The Nature Theater of Oklahoma," and "In the Penal Colony," as well as the final chapter to his novel *Amerika*, and the beginning of his unfinished novel *The Trial*. The following year, he reconciled with Felice Bauer and published "The Metamorphosis." In 1916, he wrote "The Hunter Gracchus," "A Country Doctor," and a few other stories that would later appear in his collection *A Country Doctor*. The following year, he wrote "A Report to an Academy" and "The Great Wall of China." During this year, he became engaged once again to Felice Bauer, but broke it off after being diagnosed with Tuberculosis. His health issues continued, and after contracting the Spanish Influenza on top of the existing Tuberculosis, he was admitted into a sanatorium. In 1919, Kafka published "In the Penal Colony" and the volume of stories *A Country Doctor*. It was during this year that he wrote the posthumously published but never delivered "Letter to His Father," and began his correspondence with Milena Jesenská who would become his Czech translator and with whom he would have an affair.

By 1921, Kafka made an attempt to return to work at the Workers' Accident Insurance Institute, but retired the following year due to sickness and fatigue. In 1922, he wrote and published "A Hunger Artist" and began work on another unfinished novel, *The Castle*. The following year, he met Dora Diamant, a young Hassidic woman with whom he would spend the last months of his life. Later that year he moved to Berlin to live with Dora, and it was in Berlin where he wrote "The Burrow" and became involved in Hebrew studies. During this time his health was rapidly failing him. By 1924, he moved back to Prague where he wrote "Josephine the Singer" and entered a Sanatorium near Vienna where he made the final corrections on his collection *A Hunger Artist*, and ultimately died on June 3, 1924. Franz Kafka was buried on June 11, 1924, in a Jewish Cemetery in Prague. His collection *Hunger Artist* was published not long after his death.

The Story Behind the Story

In the ninety years since its publication, "The Metamorphosis" has received an incredible amount of international scholarly attention from a number of different academic angles. In her essay "Transforming Franz Kafka's 'Metamorphosis,'" Nina Pelikan Straus touches on this vast scholarship, suggesting that

> The reasons for scholars' interest in Kafka, particularly his short masterpiece, "Metamorphosis," reflect a recognition on the part of students of religion, philosophy, psychoanalysis, political and social criticism, Marxism, and literature that Kafka's work is inexhaustible. No single interpretation invalidates or finally delivers the story's significance. Its quality of multivalency (Vieldeutigkeit) keeps us talking to each other, against each other, and to ourselves (Straus 651).[1]

In her own essay, Straus makes the case for viewing "The Metamorphosis" through a feminist lens, focusing on Gregor's sister Grete, as well as Gregor's acknowledgement of her increasing vitality and independence.

Many scholars have suggested that "The Metamorphosis" is an allegorical tale of oppression, making use of autobiographical circumstances relating to the household within which Kafka was raised—particularly his relationship with his father—and the sickness and depression that Kafka experienced throughout his life. Considerable attention has also been paid to the startling originality of the story. In Mark Spilka's essay "Kafka's Sources for The Metamorphosis," published in 1959 in *Comparative Literature*, he suggests that "Gregor Samsa is not simply the young Kafka, as critics often hold; he is also the young Dickens, the young Copperfield, even the balding Golyadkin, who wants to dance with Klara Olsufyevna, all synthesized into one regressive hero" (305).[2] In his essay, Spilka argues that "its blend of fantasy with urban realism began with Gogol and Dostoevsky...and its central situation, that of a son locked in his room and abhorred by his own family, was first devised by Dickens" (290).[3]

Kafka wrote "The Metamorphosis" in 1912, an important and productive year for Kafka who also completed "The Judgment," began work on his first novel, *Amerika*, and met Felice Bauer, the woman to whom he would twice get engaged. Although "The Metamorphosis"—not published until 1915—has received more critical attention than any of his other stories, Stanley Corngold, in his chapter "*The Metamorphosis:* Metamorphosis of the Metaphor" from his critical volume *Franz Kafka: The Necessity of Form*, suggests that "Kafka never claimed for it any special distinction" (Corngold 47).[4] Corngold cites Kafka's diaries in which he laments "I am now reading *Metamorphosis* at home and find it bad" (Kafka qtd. in Corngold 48)[5]. This is consistent with the self-consciousness and even self-loathing that Kafka experienced throughout his life, and gives credence to the long heralded story that Kafka asked his closest friend Max Brod—one of the biographers and translators of his work, as well as the primary source for Kafka's posthumously published prose—to burn his manuscripts before he died.

Some scholars, such as Michael P. Ryan, have focused on "the variety of suffering which plagued the life of Franz Kafka" (Ryan 133)[6], suggesting that this played a part in the conception of Gregor and the "The Metamorphosis." In his essay "Samsa and *Samsara*: Suffering, Death, and Rebirth in 'The Metamorphosis,'" Ryan cites Franz Kempf's view that "The Metamorphosis" "depict[s] the 'mercilessness of the world'" (133)[7]. Given the difficulties that Kafka had with his father, his health and his job, many critics have made the case that in "The Metamorphosis," Kafka was portraying a condition where one is treated and/or views oneself as less than human—an animal, an insect.

Another of Kafka's conditions that scholars have focused on relates to his feelings of shame and guilt, particularly in relation to his family. In his essay "Franz Kafka and Animals," Peter Stine suggests a connection between the use of animals—one prominent example being the dung beetle—and Kafka's veiled portrayal of his family. Stine "speculate[s] that Kafka, in turning to his family for subject matter, needed the animal world for fear of violating his own sense of wholesomeness while exploring under the rock of repression" (Stine 62)[8]. Kafka's ability to successfully join the fantastic and the real is often noted as being at the root of his genius.

The very nature of "The Metamorphosis," a work that asks its readers to accept that the protagonist has been metamorphosed into a giant dung beetle, demands an investigation of the story's events that goes beyond the surface features of plot. Since Kafka's death in 1924, many letters, diaries, pieces of fiction (finished and unfinished), parables, nonfiction prose pieces and biographical writings have surfaced, giving literary scholars ample material from which to speculate about the origins of, and interpret the events within, the rich, complex tale of "The Metamorphosis." Kafka's "Letter to His Father" details a circumstance in which he is left outside and treated as an animal, a concept that has been given life in a few of Kafka's fictions, including "The Metamorphosis." When thinking of the life and literary influences that informed Kafka's most essential work, it is important not to overlook the singular degree of invention and imagination that ultimately allowed Franz Kafka to write a story that still manages to delight, inspire, and confound the minds of scholars, students, and a vast international reading public.

Notes

1. Straus, Nina Pelikan. "Transforming Franz Kafka's 'Metamorphosis.'" In *Signs*, Vol.14, No.3 (Spring 1989): 651-667.

2. Spilka, Mark. "Kafka's Sources for 'The Metamorphosis.'" In *Comparative Literature*, Vol. 11, No. 4 (Autumn, 1959): 289-307.

3. Ibid.

4. Corngold, Stanley. "*The Metamorphosis*: Metamorphosis of the Metaphor." In *Franz Kafka: The Necessity of Form*. Ithaca: Cornell University Press, 1988, 47-89.

5. Ibid.

6. Ryan, Michael P. "Samsa and *Samsara*: Suffering, Death, and Rebirth in 'The Metamorphosis.'" In *German Quarterly*, 72.2 (Spring 1999): 133-152.

7. Ibid.

8. Stine, Peter. "Franz Kafka and Animals." In *Contemporary Literature*, Vol. 22, No.1 (Winter, 1981): 58-80.

List of Characters

Gregor Samsa is the primary character in the story. He is a commercial traveler (traveling salesman) who lives with his parents and sister in a modest apartment. The story opens with Gregor waking up late for work, only to find himself transformed into a giant dung beetle. For the majority of the story, he remains isolated in his room, an increasing burden on his family who are forced to find jobs and take on lodgers to make up for the income that Gregor had formerly provided. By the end of the story, the family have all grown stronger and more independent while Gregor, struggling in his metamorphosed state, grows increasingly weak and eventually dies.

Grete is Gregor's younger sister and the closest family member to him. Initially, she is the most sympathetic to Gregor's condition, taking on the responsibility of feeding him, but eventually she begins to see Gregor as a burden, ultimately advocating for his removal. By the end of the story, after Gregor has died, it is clear that Grete has made the most dramatic transformation: from a dependent, insecure girl, to an attractive, independent woman.

Mr. Samsa (Gregor's father) has spent the years leading up to Gregor's metamorphosis growing increasingly lethargic, lamenting the collapse of his business, and forcing his son to be the sole provider for the family. He is the most aggressive toward the metamorphosed Gregor, once even pelting him with apples. Forced back to work by Gregor's inexplicable condition, Mr. Samsa becomes a bank messenger and is required to wear a uniform to work. After taking in some lodgers to help pay the bills, Mr. Samsa shows his renewed authority by kicking them out at the end.

Mrs. Samsa (Gregor's mother) is deeply upset by her son's metamorphosis, fainting upon first sight of him, and even toward the end, resisting her own daughter's suggestion that they remove the dung beetle (Gregor) from their home. She also gets a job to help pay the bills, and following Gregor's death, develops a renewed sense of hope in the budding prospects of her daughter.

The Chief clerk comes to the house on the day of Gregor's metamorphosis to see why he has failed to show up on time. Before Gregor reveals his condition, the chief clerk responds to Gregor's refusal to open his door by ranting about Gregor's dissatisfactory performance at work. Once Gregor opens his door, the chief clerk flees from the house, leaving his walking cane behind.

The Charwoman is an older servant who is largely unaffected by Gregor's metamorphosis. She makes a point of peering into his room everyday, playfully checking up on him. In the end, she reveals that she has disposed of the dung beetle corpse and that the Samsas won't have to worry about him anymore.

The Three Lodgers come to stay at the Samsas' home after Gregor's metamorphosis. They take advantage of the Samsas' hospitality, at one point requesting that Grete play the violin for them and then moving away from boredom and dissatisfaction. When Gregor reveals himself to them, they refuse to pay the Samsas any rent, but stay on in an effort to exploit the conditions even further. Ultimately, Gregor's father kicks them out of the house.

Anna is the Samsas' first housekeeper. She leaves just after Gregor's condition is revealed.

The Cook asks to leave the Samsas' household once she becomes aware of the metamorphosed Gregor. She promises to keep his condition a secret.

Summary and Analysis

Franz Kafka's best-known story "The Metamorphosis" opens as the protagonist, Gregor Samsa, wakes up in his bedroom, only to discover that he has inexplicably metamorphosed into a giant dung beetle. As Gregor struggles to coordinate the new facets of his insect body, and come to terms with the fantastic reality that has presented itself, it is revealed to the reader—through Kafka's third person narrative—that Gregor is a traveling salesman who lives with his parents and younger sister inside a modest apartment, for which Gregor's salary is needed to pay the bills. Gregor has never been satisfied by his work, but he is burdened not only with the responsibility of rent and household bills, but also with the difficult task of paying down his parents' debt, accumulated through the collapse of his father's business.

The narrative shifts closer to Gregor's point of view as he struggles with the more pedestrian reality that he is going to be late for work, and that a confrontation with his boss will be unavoidable. He considers calling in sick, but he doesn't want to arouse suspicion, "since during his five years' employment he had not been ill once," (91)[1] and he fears his illness would be investigated. As he consumes himself with the predicament of tardiness, his mother knocks on his door and inquires about his situation. He answers in a voice "unmistakably his own…but with a persistent horrible twittering squeak behind it" (91) that he is getting up. Although his answer seems to satisfy his mother, the fact that he is still home at this late hour of the morning leads his father to bang on his bedroom door, followed by his sister, who asks to be let in.

Gregor has no intention of letting anyone in as yet, setting his mind to the reality of his metamorphosis, hoping that he is only experiencing a temporary delusion and that before long, he will be transformed back into his usual state. But as he tries to get out of bed, he is faced with the daunting task of coordinating the broad body and "numerous little legs" (92) of an overgrown insect. His initial struggles to get out of bed prove fruitless and painful, but he is determined to move before the hour gets too late and someone from his office comes to check on him. Although his attempt to rock his big body back and forth move him closer to the edge of the bed, he is not able to make it to the floor by the time the doorbell rings and the chief clerk from his office is greeted by the Samsas' servant—the servant being one of the early indications of the comfort that Gregor's hard work afforded his family. Gregor laments to himself: "What a fate, to be condemned to work for a firm where the smallest omission at once [gives] rise to the gravest suspicion!" (94). It is the irritation at the chief clerk's arrival that gives Gregor the strength to heave himself out of bed, landing hard on the bedroom floor.

Gregor's sister and father each announce—through his closed bedroom door—that the chief clerk has arrived, and the clerk himself asks Gregor to open his door. When Gregor doesn't answer, his mother assures the clerk that Gregor's not well, and that nothing is as important to him as his work. Finally Gregor claims that he's coming, but doesn't move, for fear that he'll miss what his family and his boss are discussing. Gregor's father asks that the chief clerk be allowed to enter, but Gregor refuses, eliciting a sob from his sister. The chief clerk demands to know what is wrong with Gregor, admonishing him for his abnormal behavior. When Gregor does not respond, the chief clerk suggests that Gregor's work has not been satisfactory and that his position is expendable. Gregor responds with a series of pleas and excuses, claiming that he's not well and that he can still make it to the office, all while working his body across the floor and attempting to prop himself up against the chest of drawers.

After slipping a few times, he finally stabilizes himself long enough to hear the chief clerk and his parents talking about how unintelligible his words were. Gregor's mother gets increasingly upset, yelling for her daughter Grete to get the doctor, insisting that Gregor is ill. Despite the fact that his voice is no longer clear, Gregor is comforted by the effort his family is making on his behalf. Deciding to make an earnest attempt to allow the chief clerk in, he pushes his desk chair toward the door, climbs on top and clamps his toothless, insect jaw around the key in an effort to unlock the door. Although he is pained by the effort, and some brown fluid dribbles out of his mouth, he is successful in his attempt to unlock it.

When the door opens, the chief clerk and Gregor's parents are horrified by the inexplicable sight of the giant dung beetle: Gregor's mother faints and Gregor's father begins to weep. From Gregor's vantage point, the reader is given a description of the immediate surroundings, the details of which have garnered some attention from scholars: through the window, there is a dark gray hospital building seen through the heavy rain outside; the breakfast table is set, and the reader is told of Gregor's father's tendency to stretch the morning meal out for hours over several newspapers; on the wall outside Gregor's room is a photo of him in a military outfit, "inviting one to respect his uniform and military bearing" (101). The details reveal the bleakness of the surroundings, as well as the rigid authority that Gregor's father once held, highlighting his current tendency toward apathy, which has forced Gregor to be the sole provider for the family.

Gregor tries to instigate conversation with the chief clerk, suggesting that he still plans to get dressed and make his way to the office, and despite the grind of traveling, he wouldn't want any other job. He pleads with the clerk to offer a favorable account of the situation, insisting that his condition is only temporary, that he will bounce back with greater force, and that his parents and sister depend on him to work for the family. As Gregor continues his plea, the chief clerk backs slowly toward the front door of the Samsa home, finally turning and running away as quickly as he's able. Gregor knows that he must stop the clerk from leaving if he has any hope of holding on to his position, so in an awkward effort to coordinate his new fleet of tiny legs, Gregor maneuvers out of his room and sets out after the clerk, falling on his belly from the urgency of the effort. Although he is comforted by his soft landing and his ability to maintain some control over his vast extremities—for a few yards at least—Gregor is jarred back to reality by the frantic cries coming from his mother who has backed into the kitchen table, causing the coffee pot to overturn. Gregor tries to calm his mother who is understandably frightened by the sight of a giant dung beetle with flapping jaws.

Gregor's mother finally runs into the arms of her husband who grabs the walking stick that the chief clerk had left behind and uses it to drive Gregor back toward his room. Gregor's mother opens a window and lets the cold air rush in while her husband stamps his feet and Gregor does his best to walk backward. Unable to control his backward direction, Gregor is forced to turn around and concentrate on making it to his room without disturbing his father more than necessary. When he gets there, only one side of the entryway is open. Since he can't expect anyone to open the other side for him, he attempts to leap through the narrow opening, lodging his bulky frame in the doorway, fluids from his body running over the white door. Part I concludes with a great push from his father, "a deliverance" (105) that forces Gregor into his room, punctuated by the slamming of his bedroom door.

Part II opens that evening as Gregor wakes from a deep sleep. In an effort to see what is happening outside his room, he crawls toward the door, nursing his left side, which is still in considerable pain from his earlier entry into his room. When he gets to his door, he is pleasantly surprised to find a tray of food, most likely left by his sister. Despite his considerable hunger, he is revolted by the smell and taste of the bread and milk. Thoughts of food turn to a reflection on the relative comfort that he had been able to provide for his family thus far; but his positive thoughts quickly turn dark at the possibility that his life might end in a ghastly way. To combat his anxiety, he paces around the room, hoping that someone might come in to see him. Eventually the light from the living room is turned off, and Gregor hears his family members tip-toeing to their rooms. Upset by the reality of the circumstances, Gregor wedges his body beneath the couch, desperate for comfort.

Although hunger and anxiety prevent him from falling into a deep sleep, Gregor is able to rest with adequate comfort until the early morning when his sister opens his door and peers into his room. At the sight of Gregor's body, she slams the door shut, opening it again a few moments later. Gregor watches from beneath the couch as his sister creeps into the room. At this point, the narrative dips into Gregor's point of view as he wonders: "Would she notice that he had left the milk standing, and not out of hunger, and would she bring in some other kind of food more to his taste?" (107). He resists the urge to throw himself at her feet as he watches his sister take the tray out of the room.

Much to Gregor's surprise, Grete returns with an assortment of food items, meant to determine what he might want, given his current condition. She leaves the food on the floor and retreats from the room, turning the key to indicate that he'll have adequate privacy. Gregor scampers out quickly and finds himself drawn to the cheese, vegetables and sauce, but turned off by the fresher items. After stuffing himself, his sister returns, opening the door slowly enough to allow Gregor time to hide beneath the couch. She gathers the remains into a bucket and leaves. The reader is told that this is the pattern for Gregor's meals: two times a day—in the morning and in the evening—brought in and picked up by his sister.

Since Gregor's speech is unintelligible to his family members, they do not attempt to speak to him, and he is forced to gather any information he can by listening through the door. He hears the cook's teary request to quit, swearing that she won't utter a word about the situation in the house. When she is finally relieved of her duty, Gregor's sister Grete is forced to take over the cooking duties. However the reader is told that there isn't much cooking for Grete to do since the family, in particular Gregor's mother, have not been eating much. Gregor overhears his father divulging the state of the family's finances, pulling out various articles from his small safe, most left over from the demise of his former business. The reader is told explicitly that it was the failure of his father's business that forced Gregor to "work with unusual ardor and almost overnight...become a commercial traveler" (110). Gregor's efforts in this capacity had been more than adequate, allowing him to take care of the family's expenses, and allowing his family to take his efforts for granted—evidenced most noticeably in the presence of a cleaning woman and a cook.

The reader is also made aware of Gregor's closeness with his sister, and of his "secret plan...that she, who loved music...should be sent...to study at the Conservatorium" (111). These plans, however, can not be realized in his current condition. Although he is disheartened by his thwarted dream for his sister, he is encouraged by the news—heard through the door of his room—that a few investments had made it through the collapse of his father's business, and that a certain amount of the money that he had brought home still remained.

But it is the thought of money that proves most distressing for Gregor. Although what remains could last a year or two, eventually someone will have to earn a salary, and Gregor can't imagine anyone in his family being able to work. This inability to even conceive of his family working has been the source of some literary scholarship that has focused on the parasitic relationships that exist in the Samsa home: first the family on Gregor, then Gregor on the family. Only with Gregor's death are the members of his family finally liberated, each achieving a greater sense of vitality and independence. But before the reader is taken to this stage, the current conditions are spelled out: Gregor's father hasn't worked in five years and has grown heavy, his mother has severe asthma, and his sister is only seventeen and has not done serious work in her life.

In an effort to deal with his anxiety and shame regarding his family's situation, Gregor manages to push the chair in his room near the window where he can crawl up and gaze outside. At first this provides some comfort—serving as a reminder of the freedom that exists in the world—but before long his vision starts to change, and everything outside his window appears as a large gray blur. His inability to see the outside world has also been a focus of some writing on the story, the critical lens often falling on the distortion that results from societal or even familial oppression—this with the understanding that Gregor's metamorphosis is symbolic of an oppressive state. But at this point in the story, Gregor's sister is unaware of the change in his vision, so recognizing that Gregor has pushed the chair near the window, she makes a point—whenever tidying up—to return the chair to its place.

His oppressive state is acknowledged explicitly when, through Gregor's close point of view, the reader is told "if he could have spoken to [his sister] and thanked her for all she had to do for him, he could have borne her ministrations better; as it was, they oppressed him" (113). Gregor is also uncomfortable by the fact that his sister has to open the windows before she can do anything else, as if the smell of the room is almost too revolting to bear. He is further upset when his sister opens the door and sees him gazing out the window, the sight causing her to slam the door closed, not returning until the middle of the day. Gregor responds with tremendous shame—a recurring theme throughout the story—laboring to carry a sheet across the room so he can hide the parts of himself that stick out from his hiding place beneath the couch.

At this point, the reader is told of how grateful Gregor's parents are for Grete's efforts, "whereas formerly they had frequently scolded her for being as they thought a somewhat useless daughter" (114). Gregor often hears the conversations that follow his sister's visits to his room, most of which concern his condition. Eventually, however, the conversations turn to his mother's desire to enter the room, and his father and sister's protestations. The opportunity finally comes when Grete concludes, based on the tracks that Gregor has left from his habit of crawling around the walls and the ceiling, that he would be better off without all the furniture in his room.

Not daring to ask her father for any assistance, Grete solicits her mother to help move the large, heavy objects out of Gregor's room. Grete makes sure that Gregor is well covered—hidden as completely as possible beneath the couch and the sheet—then signals for her mother to enter the room. The two women do their best to move the heavy chest, but after a quarter of an hour, they are unable to move it any significant distance. This leads to a conversation—in whispers—about whether the idea to move Gregor's furniture might indicate that they had given up on the possibility that he could return to his normal state. His mother believes that they should not move the furniture at all, but in Grete's new-found confidence, she is able to persuade her mother that moving the chest is the right thing to do, reinstating the effort to push it out of the room. This is one of the first obvious hints at the transformation that Grete is experiencing. Scholars who have viewed "The Metamorphosis" through a feminist lens, have focused considerable attention on Grete's transformation from dependant child, to independent, more self-assured adult.

Gregor initially supports Grete's idea that his room should be cleared of obstacles, but he soon becomes nostalgic over the desk and pictures and other items of memorabilia that had shaped his life up to the time of his metamorphosis. Unable to contain himself any longer, he runs out from under the couch in hopes of stopping his mother and sister from taking away any more of his furniture. When they return to the room, Gregor is clamped onto a picture on his wall, causing Grete to shield her mother from witnessing the horror that has become her son. But before her mother can be led out of the room, she sees Gregor and faints. Grete searches the apartment for smelling solutions to arouse her mother, and Gregor, in a frantic effort to assist, follows his sister out of the room, indirectly causing her to break a bottle, a shard of which cuts Gregor's face. Grete then shuts Gregor out of his room and proceeds to tend to her mother. In an effort to deal with his helplessness and worry, Gregor climbs around the walls and ceiling, eventually falling onto the living room table.

Before long, the door bell rings and Grete lets her father in, telling him that her mother had fainted and that Gregor has gotten loose. Gregor's father grows incensed by what he assumes is Gregor's wrong doing. At this point, the reader becomes aware of how much Gregor's father has changed since Gregor's metamorphosis. He has turned from a lethargic, failed businessman to a productive, active member of the work force. When Gregor sees him, he is stunned by how fit he looks, his appearance enhanced by his blue uniform with gold buttons. When his father finally sees him, a very slow chase around the living room ensues. Just as Gregor gets some distance, his father starts pelting him with apples. Part II ends as Gregor's mother runs out of Gregor's room, begging her husband to spare their son, just as Gregor loses consciousness.

Part III opens with a discussion of the serious injury inflicted on Gregor, disabling him for over a month, and leaving him with a rotten apple stuck to his body, no one willing to take it off. Despite his impaired movement, Gregor is convinced that his injury has at least reminded his family that he is not their enemy; they have even begun to leave the living room door open at night, allowing him to watch them from the darkness of his room. It is at this point when the reader is made aware of the employment that each member of the family has found—concrete signs of their respective transformations from inert dependency to active independence: Gregor's mother has found work as a seamstress for an undergarment company, his sister is working as a salesgirl while also "learning shorthand and French in the evenings on the chance of bettering herself" (123), and his father, who often falls asleep in his uniform, has become a bank messenger. In addition to their new jobs, the Samsa family has released their servant and hired "a gigantic bony charwoman with white hair flying around her head...[to]...do the rough work" (124). With the family so busy, Gregor sees himself as an increasing burden, lamenting the fact that his family members are forced to work so hard, and that they can not move to a more suitable home because of him.

Gregor becomes increasingly glum, at times wallowing in memories of his past as a commercial traveler, and other times stewing at how his family—particularly his sister—have begun to neglect him. He sees no reason for his neglect, given that the charwoman whom the family has hired shows no fear of him, and regularly opens his door and says a few words to "the old dung beetle" (127). As time goes by, Gregor grows increasingly depressed—a state that Kafka himself often struggled with. In the story, Gregor rarely eats and is forced to deal with the growing grime in his room, as well as the stray objects that the family have stored there to make room for three lodgers, described as "serious gentlemen...with full beards" (127), whom Gregor starts to resent—"'How these lodgers are stuffing themselves, and here am I dying of starvation!'" (127).

On a night when the lodgers are gorging on steak, Gregor hears—for the first time since his metamorphosis—the sound of his sister's violin coming from the kitchen. Having finished their meals, the lodgers ask if the violin can be played in the living room instead of the kitchen. Gregor's father agrees for his daughter, and the family carry the music stand, the music and Grete's violin into the living room where Grete sets up and begins to play. Excited by the sound of his sister's violin, Gregor crawls into the living room to listen. He is aware of how ghastly he must appear—so much dust and old food stuck to his body—but he doesn't care.

In the beginning of the performance, everyone is fully absorbed in the music. But after a while, the lodgers grow restless and move toward the back of the room, puffing on their cigars. Meanwhile Gregor, who is thoroughly moved by the music, inches forward, hoping to catch his sister's eye. As he crawls farther into the living room, he imagines his sister playing privately for him in his room; he imagines confessing how he had always intended to send her to the conservatorium, and imagines his sister's elated response, bursting into tears and kissing him on the neck. At the height of Gregor's fantasy, one of the lodgers sees him and points him out to Gregor's father who does his best to divert their attention from the giant dung beetle. In the commotion, Grete stops playing her violin and rushes into the lodgers' room to make their beds before her father can usher them back. Finally the lead lodger stamps his foot and announces that he plans to give notice, and that due to the unsanitary conditions, he will not pay for the time he has already spent there.

Gregor stays still as his father slumps in his chair and his mother loses hold of Grete's violin, letting it drop to the ground. Finally Grete speaks, declaring that the situation cannot go on any longer. She makes a distinction between Gregor and the creature they have been taking care of, demanding that they find a way to get rid of him. Gregor's father tries to think of some sort of agreement they might be able to work out with Gregor, but Grete is insistent that her father "must try to get rid of the idea that this is Gregor" (134). She rushes behind her father and in a frightful fury insists that the creature wants to take over their home. Gregor does his best to turn around and crawl back to his room, but in his weakened state, the process is difficult and slow. When he finally makes it back, his sister rushes to the door and locks him inside. Gregor lets his body relax and wishes that he had the power to disappear, as his sister now seems to want. But Gregor holds no ill will, and in a state of relative calm, he reflects on his family until the bell on the clock tower strikes three and he takes his final breath, sinking to the floor and dying at that exact moment.

The following morning, the charwoman arrives and goes about her noisy routine, eventually peeking into Gregor's room and trying to tickle him with the end of the broom handle. When this garners no reaction, she begins to prod him until it becomes clear that he is dead. She immediately walks to the Samsas' room, opens the door and announces Gregor's death. Grete and her parents all gather at Gregor's door to confirm that he has indeed died. Then the charwoman opens the window and shuts the door.

Before long, the three lodgers come out of their room and demand breakfast. The charwoman quiets them and points them into Gregor's room where they can see the dung beetle's corpse. Soon after, Grete and her parents emerge from the bedroom and Grete's father demands that the lodgers leave immediately, demonstrating an authority that he hasn't possessed since the collapse of his business. After a moment of protest, the lodgers leave and the family feels "as if a burden has been lifted" (138). Grete and her parents decide to take the day off from work and go outside for a stroll. As they're writing their respective letters of excuse, the charwoman announces that she has disposed of Gregor's body.

The story ends as the remaining Samsas leave the apartment together and take the train out to the countryside. They realize that their situation is more hopeful than it had once seemed. They will finally have the opportunity to move to a smaller and more manageable apartment. As they reflect on their improving state, Mr. and Mrs. Samsa become simultaneously "aware of their daughter's increasing vivacity, [and] that in spite of all the sorrow of recent times...she had bloomed into a pretty girl with a good figure" (139). They realize that the time to find her a husband is coming soon. "And it was like a confirmation of their new dreams and excellent intensions that at the end of their journey their daughter sprang to her feet first and stretched her young body" (139).

Note

1. All primary source references and citations from the following: Kafka, Franz. "The Metamorphosis," translated by Willa and Edwin Muir. In *Franz Kafka: The Complete Stories.* New York: Schocken Books, Inc., 1971: pgs. 89-139.

Critical Views

MARK M. ANDERSON ON THE BUG AS METAPHOR

This critical tendency to de-emphasize the bug's status as a visual object of representation reached its most extreme and brilliant limit in Stanley Corngold's influential essay "The Metamorphosis of the Metaphor".[4] Drawing on Anders's insight that Kafka often literalizes metaphors as the basis for his central images and plot lines, Corngold interprets Gregor's form as primarily linguistic and rhetorical rather than visual. Because the text circumvents the dialectical relationship of metaphor, insisting that Gregor is a bug but without denying him specifically human traits, the monstrous vermin form functions as a 'mutilated metaphor, uprooted from familiar language'(59), an 'opaque sign' (56). Anything disturbing about his appearance arises primarily from a disturbing use of rhetorical structure, an 'unclean' mixing of the metaphor's human tenor and its material vehicle.

> It appears, then, that the metamorphosis in the Samsa household of man into vermin is unsettling not only because vermin are disturbing, or because the vivid representation of a human 'louse' is disturbing, but because the indeterminate, fluid crossing of a human tenor and a material vehicle is in itself unsettling. (56)

Such interpretations have an indisputable hold on Kafka's story and, I suspect, are ultimately correct. Kafka knew that his story was kind of literary tease, that it depended on the reader's imagination to visualize what is only suggested by the text. When confronted with his editor's plan to illustrate the bug for the cover of the first edition, his response was unambiguous: 'The insect itself cannot be depicted' (letter of 25 October 1915). He proposed instead the image of a half-opened door with only darkness behind it—the bug itself remains unseen and the reader must perform the same act of imagination that is required by text in the passage from linguistic sign to mental image. Kafka's suggestion was in fact taken up, and a black-and-white illustration by Ottomar Starke adorned the story's first edition in Kurt Wolff's series *Die weißen Blätter*.

None the less, one cannot help feeling that such critical and authorial strictures have something of a magician's legerdemain—Now you see him, now you don't—and hide as much as they reveal. Although the text is a verbal artifact which expertly subverts the metaphorical function of language, it also requires the reader to make a sustained effort to visualize the bug within a minutely described environment. Moreover, such strictures obscure the fact that the text repeatedly displays Gregor's body as a visual object of unusual power—a scandalous, grotesque object difficult to behold, yes, but one that is attributed with an undeniable aesthetic function, as in the scene when Gregor hangs himself on the wall in front of his mother and sister. Indeed, the basic movement of all three sections of the novella consists in covering and uncovering Gregor's body, like a monster at a fair or a sacred icon.

Note

4. First Published in 1970, the essay was reprinted in an expanded version in *The Necessity of Form*, which is the edition quoted here.

STANLEY CORNGOLD ON THE DISTORTION OF METAPHOR

Kafka's metamorphosis—through aberrant literalization—of the metaphor "this man is a vermin" appears to be an intricate and comprehensive act in which one can discern three orders of significance, all of which inform *The Metamorphosis*. These meanings emerge separately as one focuses critically on three facts: that the metaphor distorted is a familiar element of ordinary language; that, the distortion being incomplete, the body of the original metaphor maintains a shadow existence within the metamorphosis, and the body of this metaphor—a verminous bug—is negative and repulsive; and finally, that the source of the metamorphosis is, properly speaking, not the familiar metaphor but a radical aesthetic intention. Together these meanings interpenetrate in a dialectical way. For example, the aesthetic intention reflects itself in a monster but does so by distorting an initially monstrous metaphor; the outcome of its destroying a negative is itself a negative. These relations illuminate both Kafka's saying, "Doing the negative thing is imposed on us, an addition" (DF 36–37), and his remark to Milena Jesenská-Pollak, "But even the truth of longing is not so much its truth, rather is it an expression of the lie of everything else" (LM 200). For the sake of analysis, each of the three intents can be separated and discussed independently.

Kafka metamorphoses a figure of speech embedded in ordinary language. The intent is to make strange the familiar, not to invent the new; Kafka's diaries for the period around 1912 show that his created metaphors are more complex than "salesmen are vermin." To stress the estrangement of the monster from his familiar setting in the metaphor—the dirty bug—is to stress Gregor Samsa's estrangement from his identity in the family. Gregor harks back to, yet defiantly resists, integration into the "ordinary language" of the family. The condition of the distorted metaphor, estranged from familiar speech, shapes the family drama of *The Metamorphosis*; the *Ungeziefer* is in the fullest sense of the word *ungeheuer* (monstrous)—a being that cannot be accommodated in a family.[18]

Is it too odd an idea to see this family drama as the conflict between ordinary language and a being having the character of an indecipherable word? It will seem less odd, at any rate, to grasp the family life of the Samsas as a characteristic language. The family defines itself by the ease with which it enters into collusion on the question of Gregor. Divisions of opinion do arise—touching, say, on the severity of the treatment due Gregor—but issue at once into new decisions. The family's projects develop within the universe of their concerns, through transparent words and gestures that communicate without effort. At the end, images of family unity survive the story: the mother and father in complete union; mother, father, and daughter emerging arm in arm from the parents' bedroom to confront the boarders; mother and father "growing quieter and communicating almost unconsciously through glances" at the sight of their good-looking, shapely daughter (M 58).

Note
18. Weinberg, *Kafkas Dichtungen*, p. 317.

George Gibian Compares *The Metamorphosis* with *The Judgment*

The elements of phantasy, nightmare and fear are much stronger in *The Metamorphosis* than in *The Judgment*. The horror of waking up transformed into an insect brings in its train all our subconscious fears of transformation (discussed among others in Freud's essay on *The Uncanny*). In *The Judgment*, we are at least temporarily in a normal world, and nothing ever happens which is completely impossible; in *The Metamorphosis* we are never placed in an everyday world. The narrative has the tone of carefully evaluating all evidence, but the family's reaction to Gregor's transformation—their effort to behave in the most rational and acceptable way—only strikes us as a frightening incongruity. It suggests to us that our own accepted world may be as unreal as that of the Samsas, and that painstaking reasonableness and conventionality may be as misplaced and vain as Gregor's and his family's. The failure of the characters to question the possibility of Gregor's metamorphosis, which is the most surprising thing of all and the basis of the action, makes the readers insecure in regard to things we consider so certain that we seldom even feel the need to think about them.

More clearly than *The Judgment*, *The Metamorphosis* moves from a beginning which ought to be a renewal of life (the awakening in the morning), but actually is moribund and catastrophic, to a conclusion which brings the death of the protagonist, accompanied by the promise of an improved life for the survivors. When we look at the line of development from Gregor's point of view, it is a steady decline leading to Gregor's extinction. When we look at it through the family's eyes, it is a long effort to contain and to eliminate Gregor and the evils he has brought about—the lodgers, the cleaning woman's attitude—a struggle which is crowned with success in the end when he dies and his body is disposed of. *The Judgment* had a similarly tight structure, with a sharply marked beginning, middle and end, but the death of the son lacked the counterpoise which it has in *The Metamorphosis*, the brightening future of the rest of the family, which shows still more clearly the son's guilt and worthlessness.[6]

The still broader parabolic meaning of *The Metamorphosis* is its greatest point of difference from *The Judgment*. If the *Letter* applies only to Kafka and his father, and *The Judgment* to the father-son relationship in general with overtones implicating other power-to-subject relations, then *The Metamorphosis* has strong suggestions of many possible interpretations. Some of the situations to which it can be taken to refer are: man and the state; man and his subconscious feelings of guilt and inadequacy in general; totemistic fears of metamorphosis; the Jew in a Gentile society; man and grace; or man and God. The mood of the story is precise, but the references made by it parabolically are multiple.

Note

6. It should be pointed out that in contradistinction to the two stories discussed here, most of Kafka's writing, his novels as well as stories, is characterized by the absence of a clearly marked conclusion. This, however, does not mean that such works are inconclusive. Their construction, unlike that of *The Judgment* and *The Metamorphosis*, is multicellular, and each cell bears its own conclusion within itself. The series as a whole therefore needs none, since each unit composing it conveys the message of the unending series. This is the point missed by those who criticize Kafka for the frequency with which he left his works unfinished. Günther Anders, *Kafka: Pro und Kantra* (Munich, 1951), pp. 34-36, has an interesting discussion of the cyclical and repetitive nature of Kafka's scenes, but errs in condemning Kafka's philosophy, besides other reasons, on the ground of his failure to complete his works. Wilhelm Emrich, "Franz Kafka," in Hermann Friedmann and Otto Mann, *Deutsche Literatur im Zwaneigsten*

Jahrbundert (Heidelberg, 1954), p. 231 and passim, discusses interestingly the infinitely continuable series of Kafka's episodes, and Paul Goodman, *The Structure of Literature* (Chicago, 1954), pp. 173-183, analyzes the cellular structure of *The Castle*.

M. Elizabeth Macandrew on the Father/Son Reversal

Literalized metaphor permits Kafka the same sort of Flexibility that it gave to Swift. Gregor's father and sister are also transformed in the course of the story, but, as we shall see, in them the change is less permanent than in Gregor. Consequently, Kafka treats it figuratively, not literally. As Gregor's humiliation deepens and his father's self-confidence and self-respect grow, we begin to understand what really makes Gregor an insect. He has gained a moral ascendancy over his father, who, his business having failed, sits around the house or dodders helplessly about, supported by cane. Gregor has become the pillar of the household, paying the debts and planning to send his sister to the conservatory. But he is a mere insect of a man, quite incapable of dominating anyone for long. The roles of father and son reverse themselves, the son becoming an insignificant insect hiding in corners, the father, self-confident in his bank messenger's uniform, driving him away.

We can assume from the exactness of the reversal that father and son are much alike—weak men, both, who feel the need of a front with which to face the world. For each, a precariously held status is symbolized in a uniform. When Gregor emerges from his room that first morning, his eyes fall at once on "a photograph of himself on military service...a carefree smile on his face, *inviting one to respect his uniform and military bearing*" (p. 82, my italics). Similarly, the father, once he has succeeded in dominating his son again, wears his uniform even in the house. "He slept [we are told] fully dressed where he sat, as if he were ready for service at any moment and even here only at the beck and call of his superior" (p.111). He is now at the point at which Gregor was as a salesman, as we saw when he pleaded with the chief clerk, "I'm loyally bound to serve the chief, you know that very well" (p.82).

As the struggle between the two unfolds, we begin to find there is a contrast between the patient, self-sacrificing son who has rescued his helpless father from disaster (this is Gregor's version) and that same son timidly fleeing, without thought of resistance, without even anger, before the wrath of his aggressive father, who turns out to be quite capable of taking over again his position as head of the family (this is the action). And because of this contradiction we suspect Gregor's motives in making his self-sacrifice.

The scene in which Gregor's father wounds him is very detailed and reveals the psychological situation. Gregor looks at his father and "truly, this was not the father he had imagined to himself...The man who used to lie wearily sunk in bed...who could not really rise to his feet...Now he was standing there in fine shape; dressed in a smart blue uniform with gold buttons" (p. 107f). Gregor flees and the father chases him, then bombards him with apples. One "landed right on his back and sank in; Gregor wanted to drag himself forward, as if this startling, incredible pain could be left behind him...With his last conscious look he saw...his mother...in her underbodice...rushing towards his father, leaving one after another behind her on the floor her loosened petticoats, stumbling over her petticoats straight to his father and embracing him in complete union with him—but here Gregor's sight began to fail—with her hands clasped round his father's neck as she begged for her son's life" (p. 109f).

Having been brought to this scene armed largely with Gregor's view of the situation, we can hardly fail to share his bewilderment at this sudden revelation of the father's violence, but we, being readers, begin to make adjustments which Gregor cannot make, to understand what this bewilderment reveals about him as well as what it tells us about his father. When Gregor faints, shutting out the complete union of his parents, our sympathies are still with him. But our understanding has gone far beyond his. It is conflict with his father that makes Gregor a beetle, not being a salesman; that only made him conscious of it. The wounding re-reverses the roles exactly; "his injury had impaired, probably for ever, his powers of movement, and for the time being it took him long, long minutes *to creep across his room like an old invalid*" (p. 110, my italics). Gregor is now in the state his father was in at the beginning of the story.

PHILIP H. RHEIN COMPARES KAFKA WITH ARTIST ALFRED KUBIN

Everyone is familiar enough with the uniqueness of the Kafka and Kubin world, a world from which the reader or viewer is often alienated by fantastic objects and events. Logic as we ordinarily speak of it has no meaning in this world that lies beyond the limits of man's workaday experience, if not beyond man's understanding. It is not a fairy-tale world of dreams, but a world of dreams in which enough reality is retained that the reader or viewer is forced to acknowledge its familiarity. Gregor in Kafka's *The Metamorphosis* (1915) or Death in Kubin's *The Painter* (1918) are obviously unreal figures in the ordinary world; yet both are treated in terms of the clearest, most concise logic. They *are*. The logical treatment of the unreal, so obvious in these instances, is true for all of Kafka's writings and Kubin's drawings. Once the original situation is accepted, the dénouement follows in the most logical manner.

The world as revealed by Kafka and Kubin is a product of their personal, inner experience; and because of their persistent preoccupation with the details and clutter of the real world, we are forced to be concerned with the living, the human, and the real in an apparently unreal situation. This emphasis upon detail is most significant when we are aware of the economy of expression employed by both artists. Nowhere are we bogged down under a torrent of needless verbal or visual description. The minutiae of the real world are retained as a point of contact between our reality and the suprareality of the art products and as an environmental backdrop to unreal or strange characters who are misfits in an otherwise fluid situation. The reader or viewer is constantly tossed between the extremes of reality and unreality which are on the point of meeting but never meet.

On one level, Kafka's and Kubin's works express keen psychological observation and social criticism; but beneath this surface level, they seek to shape a metaphysical experience through which a man may find his freedom from time and actuality. They do not pretend that modern life is beautiful and humane; their intent is quite different. They do not seek to resolve man's social problems but rather to release man from them so that he can attain a level of understanding that transcends the imposed limits of time and space.

This world that they create is an abstract world; not abstract in the way that science is abstract, but abstract in that it deals only with the essential. Here the personal problem no longer exists, and that which seems still personal, is the very moment it is uttered, dissolved into the realm of myth. Kafka and Kubin succeed in projecting the personal problems of the individual into the realm of the universal problems of men. In a work by either of the men, the initially private problem of the piece is extended and modified until it no longer exists on the purely personal level. By means of the artist's selection and manipulation of material, the personal evolves into the suprapersonal, and the problems of the individual are superseded by the problems of man. Camus, in writing about Kafka, stated that, "His work is universal to the extent to which it represents the emotionally moving face of man fleeing humanity, deriving from his contradictions reasons for believing, reasons for hoping from his fecund despair and calling life his terrifying apprenticeship in death."[3] Camus' statement is equally applicable to the art of Kubin.

As we move from the ideological world that frames the works of Kafka and Kubin into the particular world that is locked within that frame, we enter a world of language and line that is systematically ordered and controlled with absolute precision. In *The Metamorphosis* by Kafka and *The Painter* by Kubin, the ideological similarities of the two artists are underscored by the election and arrangement of details that serve to guide the reader or viewer of these works. To begin at the beginning, the titles themselves invite speculation. Just as the transformation of the commercial traveler Gregor Samsa is completed in the first sentence of the Kafka story, so too is the death of the painter an obvious and immediately conveyed visual fact of Kubin's pencil drawing. Gregor's metamorphosis and the painter's death are the unquestionable givens of the two art products, and these facts are never doubted by the reader or viewer. Unlike the pattern of traditional analytic tragedy in which the questions of guilt and innocence are raised and resolved, these questions are never addressed by either Kafka or Kubin. Paradoxically, however, these same questions become the central concern of the reader or viewer as he seeks to untangle the meaning of the presented details. The initial problem is further complicated by an additional given fact. The ambiguity of the titles emphasizes the impossibility of any facile interpretation of either the story or the drawing. Obviously, the metamorphosis of Gregor and the death of the painter are accomplished acts; however, the title of the Kafka story might apply to Gregor's sister, Grete, with more justification than to Gregor himself, for it is, after all, her metamorphosis that is revealed in the unfolding of the narrative. The title of the Kubin drawing is equally ambiguous. On first glance, the painter of the title seemingly refers to the lifeless human form that lies before the canvas; yet the linear arrangement of details within the drawing quickly moves the viewer's eyes to the central figure of death, here portrayed with an artist's palette in his hand, completing the as yet unfinished canvas. Death is the focal point of the drawing; and he, like Grete in *The Metamorphosis*, is the figure we witness acting out the drama of the composition.

The movement inherent within the two art works is also comparable. The Kafka or Kubin character is brought into the conflict between the world of everyday life and the world of supernatural anxiety. As he moves more deeply into this conflict, no problem is resolved; everything begins over and over again. He attempts to capture meaning through what negates that meanings, but he is constantly thrown back upon himself, upon the one thing that has no definition. He is caught in the circular movement of a whirlpool that inevitably sucks him under. This circular movement is emphasized in *The Metamorphosis* by Gregor's perpetual motion that never budges him from the spot. The circle that forms the frame of the story by enclosing the action between two metamorphoses is repeated internally in several ways. In the first part of *The Metamorphosis*, the constant ticking of the alarm clock symbolically reflects the irrevocable circle of Gregor's past life as a traveling salesman, locked into the world of clock time. Later in the story, when specific time no longer has any meaning in Gregor's world, the alarm clock disappears and is replaced by Gregor's own ceaseless, atemporal, circular movement that binds him within a world that is no longer understood or measured realistically. Finally, Gregor's aimless circular wanderings are halted by the round apples that are embedded in his hard shell. Through Gregor's death, temporal order is restored, the shapeless vagueness that permeates the story is eradicated and the circle of the metamorphosis is completed.

Notes
3. David Eggenschwiler. "*The Metamorphosis*, Freud, and the Chains of Odysseus," in *Franz Kafka*, ed. Harold Bloom (New York: Chelsea House, 1986), 199–219.

MICHAEL ROWE ON THEMES IN *THE METAMORPHOSIS*

The critical literature on *Metamorphosis* is voluminous and wide ranging. Themes in the story include, among myriad others, incest, rebellion against the father, and family shame;[7] socioeconomic and social class critiques;[8] and isolation and alienation,[9] More relevant for this essay are discussions by such writers as R. D. Luke, Paul Landsberg, and Robert Coles about the story's symbolism, in which physical transformation may metaphorically represent psychological or spiritual transformation.[10] Illness threatens not only the individual's physical integrity but also the individual's identity and sense of self in the world, as Eric Cassell writes: "Persons do things. They act, create, make, take apart, put together, wind, unwind …When illness makes it impossible for people to do these things, they are not themselves." [11] Not only are those who fall ill "not themselves" from their own point of view; they are not themselves to others, or, at the very least, others have trouble seeing the "self" they have known in the past in the ill person they see before them in the present.

Although becoming an insect is not quite a disease, Gregor's transformed identity, in which his taken-for-granted life is suddenly disrupted,[12] may be likened to the onset of serious physical or mental illness. Serious illness damages the person not only in fact but also in self-perception when others confirm this damage without giving comfort or demonstrating their acceptance of the changed person (or even, perhaps, when they do). As a result of both self-perception and perception of others, the person experiences the "spoiled identity" of the stigmatized, [13] in the words of Erving Goffman, and becomes an "other."

Also relevant for this essay are those commentaries on the actions of Gregor's family members. As Coles writes, "*Metamorphosis* asks us to consider not only Gregor's deadly transformation but our own continuing experience as survivors: Do we profit handily from the human degradation of others? Is our comfort earned at the expense of terrible suffering? If so, what happens to us, what metamorphosis falls upon us?"[14] Luke suggests that the story "casts dreadful and tragic light on human incapacity to appreciate disaster."[15]

Four themes in Metamorphosis are particularly relevant to my concerns. The first is a dual sundering of Gregor's humanity and of his function within his family and society due to this inability to maintain his employment. Gregor's humanity, to the extent that his parents and sister acknowledge it, is inextricably tied to his function as economic provider. When his metamorphosis makes it impossible for him to perform his job, his humanity, in the eyes of those closest to him, is threatened as well.

The second is the power and ambiguity of the function of caregiver, a theme that is likely to give pause to readers who have stood on either side of the patient-caregiver relationship. Grete, closest to Gregor in the family, naturally assumes the position of his caretaker, but she is also the first to rebel against the burden that Gregor's transformation has imposed on the family and to put up a barrier between him and any mercy he might hope to receive from his parents. For his part, Gregor is, at first, grateful to his sister for her ministrations; then he resents his dependence on her and later resents her neglect of him. In addition, Gregor has fantasies of stealing her away from the others and becoming her sold protector. This fantasy, whatever sexual connotations it has, also involves reversing the power relationship between them.

The third thematic concern is the temporal nature of the changes precipitated by Gregor's illness. While Kafka's portrayal of family relationship in the novella is almost uniformly grim, there is a gradual movement away, and finally an exclusion of Gregor, from the family circle. This inexorable movement is prompted in part by economic concerns, since Gregor's family members have to turn much of their attention to bringing in income to replace his, but it is largely an emotional movement away from him and growing denial of his humanity.

The fourth thematic interest is Gregor's continued efforts toward autonomy. Gregor's attempts to escape his dependent role—first when he tries to protect his furniture from his sister's zeal and later when he leaves his room—precipitate his injury and, finally, death. Even the most loving of caregivers might wince at this description, recognizing the difficulty of alternating between roles of "total caretaker" and equal partner.

Notes

7. See F.D. Luke, *"The Metamorphosis,"* in *Franz Kafka Today,* ed. Angel Flores and Homer Swander (Madison: University of Wisconsin Press, 1958), 25–44; Richard H. Lawson, *Franz Kafka* (New York: Unger , 1987); Paul L. Landsberg, *"The Metamorphosis"* in *The Kafka*

Problem, ed. Angel Flores (New York: Octogon, 1963), 129–140;Kohnke; and Eggenschwiler.

8. Ritchie Robertson, "On *The Metamorphosis* and the America Novel," in *Kafka: The Metamorphosis, The Trial, and The Castle* (London Longman, 1995), 157–163; Coles; and Landsberg.

9. Vladimir Nabokov, "Franz Kafka: *The Metamorphosis,*" in *Vladimir Nabokov's Lectures on Literature,* ed. Fredson Bowers (New York: Harcourt Brace Jovanovich, 1980), 251–283; Martin Greenberg, *The Terror of Art: Kafka and Modern Literature* (New York: Basic, 1968); Hartmut Bohme, "Mother Milena; On Kafka's Narcissism," in *The Kafka Debate: New Perspectives for Our Time,* ed. Angel Flores (New York: Gordian Press, 1977), 80–90, Kohnke; Lawson; and Landsberg.

10. See Luke Landsberg; Coles. See also Jack Coutchan, "Franz Kafka: The Metamorphosis," *Medical Humanitites Literature, Arts and Medicine* website. http//endeavor.med.nyu.edu/lit.med-db/webdocs/webdescrips/kafka98-des.html (New York University, 1997)

11. Eric J. Cassell, *The Nature of Suffering and the Goals of Medicine* (New York: Oxford University Press, 1991), 41.

12. Bohme; Landsberg.

13. Erving Goffman, *Stigma: Notes on the Management of Spoiled Identity* (New York: J. Aronson, 1974).

14. Coles, 311-312.

15. Luke, 33.

MICHAEL P. RYAN ON THE NAME SAMSA

In Kafka scholarship there is often a tendency toward Judaic and/or Christian interpretation. Adding *Samsara* (Hinduism, Buddhism) to Weinberg's Judaic and Christian mix, might suggest the metamorphosis of world religions. It could be viewed as an ecumenical movement; each religion working in tandem, making its contribution to "Die Verwandlung," Kafka's interest in and struggle with "religion" could also emphasize each faith's antagonism toward the other. Gregor's last name, though, passed on from generation to generation, suggests the longevity and prevalence of *Samsara.* If there is to be an overview of the possible world religions in "Die Verwandlung," it might hinge on *Samsara's* emphasis on suffering via transmigration.

Having said that, the question remains: does Kafka actually feel "alone" or does he feel trapped within a horrible cycle? Kafka tells us "my writings were about you" (Father 25); thus he may not be alone. Quite the contrary, he may be constantly followed, haunted by the oppressive image of his father. Considering Kafka's entire body of works, we are presented with an author who takes the role of something one might term transcendent. "Die Verwandlung" serves beautifully as an example; as in so many of his other stories, the main character appears to be Franz Kafka; that is why we have "K" in *Der Prozeß*, Bende-mann in "Das Urteil," and in this case Samsa. Kafka himself considers the similarity between Georg Bendemann's name and his own. He writes, "Georg has the same number of letters as Franz. In Bendemann, 'mann' is a strengthening of 'Bende'...But Bende has exactly the same number of letters as Kafka, and the vowel *e* occurs in the same places as does the vowel *a* in Kafka" (*Diaries* 214). In his works he transcends his existence as merely the author; it is a transmigration of his "soul" into new lives and bodies. He thus watches himself in this new life, his father once again stalking him within, causing suffering and a consequent death, whether by suicide or slow starvation. And as he dies within each story, Kafka views himself reborn in another, whether as a man recalling his "apehood" (Kafka, *Report* 281), a dog in "Forschungen eines Hundes" (Investigations of a Dog"), or vermin in "Die Verwandlung," The same torturous cycle then begins once again. This is why *Samsara*, denoting rebirth and suffering, is so fitting; with this term Kafka tells us what Gregor Samsa is atoning for, as "Das Urteil" came out of Kafka like a real birth, covered with filth and slime," and as the brown liquid drips from Gregor Samsa, we know this vermin might be the rebirth of that first slimy conception (*Diaries* 214). It may be Georg Bendemann, also known as Gregor Samsa, atoning for his suicide.

According to Holland, Gregor ("Samson") saves the Samsa family "("the chosen people") from the three boarders ("the Philistines") (148–49). Apart from the story of Samson in Judges, Holland states, "in fact, a good deal of incidental imagery of 'Metamorphosis' was derived from Isaiah" (14). Reading "Die Verwandlung," however, one does not find much similarity between Gregor and Samson. Samson possesses great strength; Gregor does not have the strength to get out of bed, he must swing "himself out of bed with all his might" (Kafka, "Metamorphosis" 125). Moreover, even if Gregor did possess extraordinary strength, unlike Samson there is no long hair to be cut. Similarly, Gregor does not appear to be, like Samson, a judge of Israel. Nor does the family's treatment of Gregor correspond to Samson's familial relationship. Gregor is left in his room with rotten food, and repeatedly driven back into his den of misery by his father. Samson's family is at his disposal; when he wants to marry a particular woman his family is happy to support him. Holland, however, does not suggest that "Die Verwandlung" is an inversion of the story of Samson; rather, he draws on an analogy. He writes, "Samson's sacrifice is a traditional analogue to Christ's; in German he is called *Judenchrist*" (149). Weinberg and Holland agree that "Kafka has given Gregor a number of Christ-like attributes" (Holland 147). Weinberg refers to Gregor as "*Christkind,*" and surmises that Gregor's metamorphosis is related to his desire to send his sister to *conservatoire* (237). There does appear to be something ontological about Gregor. Furthermore, *Samsara's* emphasis on suffering and rebirth could allow for such an interpretation; but there are other possibilities. Gregor's savior quality might be explained by eastern philosophy's notion of the *avatar*. This will be discussed in further detail later.

Note

This article owes a deep debt of gratitude to David H. Chisholm, Professor of German Studies, University of Arizona, for his invaluable insight, editing, and scholarly criticism. I also thank Elisabeth Neiss Cobbs, University of Arizona, for her patient editing, and *The German Quarterly's* reviewers for their thought-provoking suggestions.

Works Cited

Holland, Norman. "Realism and Unrealism: Kafka's 'Metamorphosis'" *Modern Fiction Studies* 6 (1958): 143–50.

Kafka, Franz. *Dearest Father: Stories and Other Writings*. Ed. and Trans. Ernst Kaiser and Eithne Wilkins. New York: Shocken, 1954.

———. *Franz Kafka: The Diaries 1910–1923*. Ed. Max Brod. Trans. Joseph Kresh (1910–13) and Martin Greenberg with the cooperation of Hannah Arendt (1914–23). New York: Shocken, 1976.

———. "The Metamorphosis." *The Great Short Works of Franz Kafka: The Metamorphosis, In the Penal Colony and Other Stories.* Trans. Joachim Neugroschel. New York: Simon and Schuster, 1995. 117–88. References follow this text.

———. "Report for an Academy." *The Great Short Works of Franz Kafka: The Metamorphosis, In the Penal Colony and Other Stories.* Trans. Joachim Neugroschel. New York: Simon and Schuster, 1995. 281–93. References follow this text.

Weinberg, Kurt. *Kafkas Dichtungen: Die Travestein des Mythos*. Berne: Francke, 1963.

MARK SPILKA ON KAFKA'S PREDECESSORS

Kafka's genius must then be gauged, like that of other authors, in terms of influence and tradition. The question is: In terms of what tradition? Philip Rahv defines it, ideologically, as a tendency "against scientific rationalism, against civilization, against the heresies of the man of the city whose penalty is spiritual death"; in Kafka, the tendency is balanced by an even greater stress on the humanity of the dying hero, regardless of his heresies. This leaves him still a formal innovator, in Rahv's words, an idiosyncratic writer who "departed from the norms of the literary imagination."[3] Actually there is nothing idiosyncratic about Kafka's genius; in form and content, he belongs to a special order of the urban grotesque, with its roots in German romanticism of the early nineteenth century and in Russian and English realism of the middle decades.

Consider the origin of his great short novel, *The Metamorphosis*. It was written in the fall of 1912, along with "The Judgment" and the early chapters of *Amerika*, in a veritable burst of "imitative" writing. Its basic method, that of psychological fantasy, had been anticipated by Hoffmann in the early 1800s; its blend of fantasy with urban realism began with Gogol and Dostoevsky in succeeding decades; and its central situation, that of a son locked in his room and abhorred by his own family, was first devised by Dickens at mid-century. In effect, these writers formed a literary trend, which Kafka brought to full fruition or perhaps brought into being with his story, as he synthesized and clarified the latent form. To trace the origins of *The Metamorphosis* is to establish the existence of this trend, to place Kafka well within it, and to link him especially with two other masters of the genre, Dickens and Dostoevsky, who provided the immediate sources for his story.

The trail begins with E.T.A. Hoffman, a German romantic who was fascinated with doubles. This was a familiar theme in German literature, one of the first foreshadowings of the modern concept of the unconscious. To enhance the theme, Hoffmann added the principle of hostility between doubles, or the conflict of perverse and evil impulses with the most intense idealism. His own divided nature provided the insight. As a legal councilor in Berlin and Warsaw, he knew the drabness, poverty, and obtuseness of the bureaucratic world. At the same time he tried to escape that world through lyric and imaginative flights in art and music. He tried to lead two lives, and became himself perverse and hostile in the process. But, instead of presenting that split directly in terms of his own experience, he projected it into the realm of fairy tale and fantasy. His doubles lived on a superearthly plane, in country inns and castles; they remained cut off, as it were, from their social and psychic origins, except for passing contact with the urban scene. It took a dose or two of Russian realism to bring them down to earth again, and back to their proper quarters; and, aptly enough, it took another frustrated idealist, Nikolai Gogol, to administer the first dose.

Gogol too was familiar with bureaucracy, having served for a time as a government clerk in St. Petersburg. But, instead of suppressing his experience, he used it to depict the insignificant lives of office drudges. He was the first to give careful and sympathetic attention to such types, the first to expose the squalor and banality of their existence. According to one critic, he was a romantic pessimist who fought ugliness in a peculiar way, by recording it in minute detail.[4] On his romantic side, he was attracted to Hoffman; but as a pessimist he was skeptical of Hoffman's buoyant and exotic manner—he liked to parody him by shifting his magic events to urban settings and exploiting their comic possibilities. Thus, in "The Nose," he directly spoofs the double theme in Hoffman.

In the second chapter of this tale, a lowly clerk awakens, stretches, and looks in the mirror for a pimple which had broken out on his nose the night before. To his astonishment his nose is gone. He pinches himself to make sure he is not asleep ("But no; he was no longer asleep"), and then leaps from his bed and begins to search for the missing organ. Later on his nose turns up as an independent being, a grandly dressed state councilor, the embodiment of his snobbery and sexual longing. Gogol archly concludes that "the strangest, most unintelligible fact of all is that authors actually can select such occurrences for their subject!" Without thinking much about it, he had changed the setting to satirize Hoffmann's favorite subject. But there was one perceptive reader, Dostoevsky, who took this transfer seriously. He admired Hoffman as a brilliant psychologist, but saw also that his doubles *belonged* in the urban world which had produced them; that they were more at home, as it were, in flats and offices than in country inns and castles. Accordingly, when he wrote his second novel, he restored the double to his proper dignity, and kept him in his proper quarters.

This second novel, called *The Double*, was based conceptually on "The Nose," but owed much to other tales by Gogol and Hoffmann. By a curious fluke of scholarship, two modern critics have skipped over these connections and compared "The Nose" with the opening of *The Metamorphosis*, where a young commercial traveler, Gregor Samsa wakes up in the shape of a giant insect.[5] But Kafka followed *The Double* in his story; it was Dostoevsky who followed Gogol. If we restore the missing link, we can see how an original image, rather farcical and slight, gains force and power through brilliant imitation. Consider the opening of *The Double*, in the light of Gogol's comic image; but at the same time, keep Kafka's insect well in mind. I have italicized the lines derived from Gogol.

It was a little before eight o'clock in the morning when Yakov Petrovitch Golyadkin, a titular councilor, woke up from a long sleep. He yawned, stretched, and at last opened his eyes completely. For two minutes, however, he lay in bed without moving, as though he were not yet quite certain *whether he were awake or still asleep,* whether all that was going on around him were real and actual, or the continuation of his confused dreams. Very soon , however, Mr. Golyadkin's senses began....to receive their habitual and everyday impressions. The dirty green, smoke begrimed, dusty walls of his little room, with the mahogany chest drawers and chairs, the table painted red...and the clothes taken off in haste overnight and flung in a crumpled heap on the sofa, looked at him familiarly. At last the damp autumn day, muggy and dirty, peeped into the room through the dingy window with such a hostile, sour grimace that Mr. Golyadkin could not possibly doubt that he was not in the land of Nod, but in the city of Petersburg, in his own flat on the fourth story of a huge block of buildings in Shestilavotchny Street. When he had made this important discovery Mr. Golyadkin nervously closed his eyes, as though regretting his dream and wanting to go back to it for a moment. *But a minute later he leapt out of bed at one bound, [and] ran straight to a little round looking-glass that stood on his chest of drawers...*"What a thing it would be," said Mr. Golyadkin in an undertone."*...if I were not up to the mark today, if something were amiss, if some intrusive pimple had made its appearance, or anything else unpleasant had happened;* so far, however, there's nothing wrong, so far everything's all right."

But everything is far from all right, for Golyadkin is a dual personality—by the end of the day a double appears before him, a man who looks exactly like him, who even bears his name, and who plainly figures forth his illness. Here, then, is the intrusive pimple, the unpleasant outgrowth from within, which first erupts in Gogol's minor farce, and again in Kafka's powerful novella.

Notes

3. *Op.Cit.*, p. 121.

4. Janko Lavrin, ed., *Stories from St. Petersburg*, by Nikolai Gogol (London, 1945), p. 8.

5. Victor Erlich, "Gogol and Kafka," in F*or Roman Jakobson*, ed. Morris Halle, et al, (The Hague, 1956). pp. 100–108; and T.F. Parry, "Kafka and Gogol," *German Life and Letters*, VI (1953), 141–145. Both scholars ignore the parody element in "The Nose" and credit Gogol with profound psychological intentions; but Erlich sees that the tale is not "an existential disaster."

PETER STINE ON FAMILIAL RELATIONSHIPS

We might speculate that Kafka, in turning to his family for subject matter, needed the animal world for fear of violating his own sense of wholesomeness while exploring under the rock of repression. His remarks to Brod make it clear that, for him, to write out of bad or perverted passions ("I have hundreds of wrong feelings—dreadful ones—the right ones won't come—or if they do, only in rages; absolutely weak") was to let them get the upper hand.[22] Kafka's celebrated writer's block may have been the exercise of a animal world, with *The Metamorphosis* in 1912, did his imagination find its sanction. Prior to its composition, Kafka confessed to Felice that "when I didn't write, I was at once flat on the floor, fit for the dustbin,"[23] We recognize this as the fate that befalls the hero in this story, which becomes a vehicle for Kafka to review his own failure, "a general load of fear, weakness, and self-contempt" before his father, now described from the rock-bottom reality of a despicable insect, a metamorphosis that both seals the failure and disassociates him personally from any charge of disrespect. Upon completing the story, Kafka is reported to have buoyantly asked of a friend on the streets of

Prague, "What do you think of the terrible things that go on in our family?"[24]

In *The Metamorphosis*, then, Kafka grieves about living under the invisible constraints of a family, and the enabling condition is Gregor Samsa's metamorphosis into a gigantic insect: "It was no dream."[25] Gregor's body is so alien to him that his transformation has no effect upon his mental life, which initially sets in motion droll and terrible ironies. Gregor imagines his family will take his change "calmly, he had no reason to be upset" (p. 98); he need only "put [his] clothes on" and race tardily to the office. Once in control of his legs, he breaks forth into the normal world where his eager enslavement to routine evokes a wonderful "Ugh!" as the chief clerk vanishes down the stairs. It is only when his Father drives this literalization of "troubled dreams" into his room with a newspaper—"Shoo!"—and locks him there as a prisoner, a more forcible and telescoped version of his life as son and servant of officialdom, that Gregor starts to touch reality. Indeed, his metamorphosis is less a tragedy than a naked clarification of all Gregor's relations to the world, a restoration of Truth—in particular, the hidden rage of the Father who has been battering on him like an insect.

And yet Gregor is as far removed from this "dazzling" recognition as the gap between his consciousness and his numerous waving legs. having toiled for years to bail his parents out of debt, he now feels "guilt and shame" (p. 112) that they must work and finds "cheerful" the news that his father has been duplicitous about finances and has been hoarding his son's contributions. There might be hope had Gregor experienced anger, had he in fact been guilty of the venality the chief clerk accused him of earlier, but he has no individual thoughts apart from his filial loyalty. Aware of being increasingly comfortable with his state of insecthood as he crawls the walls, Gregor need only hear his Mother talk wistfully of his old desk to renounce this adjustment. The fear of losing "all recollection of his human background" (p. 116) will culminate in his obedience to his Father's wish that he die out of simple consideration. Kafka wrote of his father that "perhaps the strangest of all my relationships with him is that I am capable of feeling and suffering to the utmost not with him, *but within him*"[26] For Gregor and for his creator metamorphosis is a kind of secret rescue from the loss of self into others, the attending alienation a form of liberation even if it does no good.

Notes

22. Brod. p. 75

23. *I am a Memory Come Alive, p. 55*.

24. Quoted by Erich Heller in his *Franz Kafka*, Modern Masters Series, Viking. p.1.

25. *Franz Kafka: The Complete Stories*, ed. Nahum N. Glatzer (New York: Schocken Paperback, 1971). p.89. All page references in the text refer to this edition.

26. *I am a Memory Come Alive*. p. 93.

ALLEN THIHER ON MISREPRESENTATION IN *THE METAMORPHOSIS*

Objects—pictures, newspapers, food—function by representing within the text the inadequacy, if not the breakdown, of representation. This concern with representation also informs much of the way in which the Kafkan narrative unfolds; events, attitudes, suppositions in "The Metamorphosis" are largely grounded in misrepresentations. For example, after Gregor awakes at the story's beginning, he misrepresents his situation to himself. He struggles to get up and catch a train, wanting to believe that his newly acquired body is no more than a passing affliction, like a cold; and at the end of the story he still dreams at times of taking up his job again, of how with the next opening of the door he might "take the family's affairs in hand just as he used to do" (125). The reader also learns, after Gregor's awakening reflection on his situation, that he may have misrepresented his job security. As the head clerk storms about before Gregor's closed door, he yells that neither Gregor's security nor his reputation are as good as Gregor thinks. These are not Gregor's only delusions. It would appear that his family's situation, its capacity to get along without him and to fend for itself, has been misrepresented to Gregor. His father, it later appears, has some money set aside, and they are all capable of working diligently to make ends meet.

The "Judgment" and "The Metamorphosis"

These misrepresentations are revealed in various ways, but especially by metamorphoses, as we see when Gregor, who is about to be judged by his father at the end of the second part, looks up from his vermin's point of view and sees the man looming above him in his new uniform. This sickly father, who, Gregor thought, was not capable of getting up in the evening, is suddenly a transformed man, or, as Gregor notes in astonishment, this was not the father he had imagined to himself. "Now, however, he stood quite straight up, wearing a tight, blue uniform with gold buttons, such as attendants in banks wear. Over the high stiff collar of his coat flowed his strong double chin. From under his bushy eyebrows pierced forward sharply and attentively the stare of his dark eyes. His usually disheveled white hair was combed down and parted in a meticulous and precise glistening hair-style" (modified translation of p.121).

Like Georg in "The Judgment," Gregor has been guilty of misrepresentations, and perhaps it is this implicit guilt that underlies the hero's fall and transforms Gregor's father, like Georg's, into a judge, into a being of strength who can now march on the once dominant son. There is no stability in this tale of metamorphosis, however; none of the representations or misrepresentations are certain and in the third part of the story the father appears to have lost much of his power. He again undergoes a metamorphosis as he sleeps evenings in his uniform, soiling his coat, and becomes another victim of the *Dreck* that covers everything. (Recall his appearance at the story's "happy end.")

In the third part of the story, however, the key and exemplary misrepresentation turns primarily on the sister. As a prelude to his disappearance, Gregor indulges in a final fantasy representation when he wants to bring his sister into his room.

Having hungered after the sustenance her violin playing promises, longing for a spiritual nourishment that this parasite without language cannot name, Gregor imagines how he might give affectionate solace to his sister after her playing is rejected by the three boarders. This fantasy of solace, whose incestuous overtones continue a parody of sexual thematics, finds its counterpart in Grete's final interpretation of the vermin. As she tells her mother and father: "You must just try to get rid of the idea that this is Gregor. The fact that we've believed it for so long is the root of all our trouble. But how can it be Gregor? If this were Gregor, he would have realized long ago that human beings can't live with such a creature…"(134). Grete's interpretation is both true and false. Kafka is wreaking havoc on the law of identity with the dialectic of misrepresentation. By applying throughout the story the kind of dream logic that allows one to be and not to be the same thing, to be Gregor and to be non-Gregor the vermin, Kafka creates the possibility for paradoxical misrepresentation at every level in "The Metamorphosis." And one may well see in this suspension of the law of identity, if one wishes, a characterization of our contemporary plight.

Works By Franz Kafka

Meditation, 1912.

The Stoker: A Fragment, 1913.

The Metamorphosis, 1915.

The Judgment, 1916.

In the Penal Colony, 1919.

A Country Doctor, 1919.

A Hunger Artist: Four Stories, 1924.

The Trial, 1925.

The Castle, 1926.

Amerika, 1927.

The Great Wall of China, 1931.

The Great Wall of China and Other Pieces, 1933.

Before the Law, 1934.

Short Stories and Short Prose Pieces, 1935.

Description of a Struggle, 1936.

Parables, 1947.

In the Penal Settlement: Tales and Short Prose Works, 1949.

The Judgment and Other Stories, 1952.

Short Stories, 1952.

Wedding Preparations in the Country and Other Posthumous Prose, 1953.

Dearest Father: Stories and Other Writings, 1954.

Short Stories and Sketches, 1959.

He, 1963.

Collected Short Stories, 1970.

The Complete Short Stories, 1971.

The Metamorphosis: A Critical Edition, 1972.

I Am a Memory Come Alive, 1974.

Annotated Bibliography

Adelman, Gary. "Beckett and Kafka." In *TriQuarterly* 117 (Fall 2003): 77–107.

In this essay, Gary Adelman discusses the crossing influences found in the work of Franz Kafka and Samuel Beckett. He addresses several works by Kafka, including "The Metamorphosis," and tries to locate each work's presence in Beckett's fiction, poetry and drama.

Alter, Robert. "Kafka as Kabbalist." In *Salmagundi* No. 98-99 (Spring-Summer 1993): 86–100.

In this essay, Robert Alter traces the Jewish mystic tradition that can be found in Kafka's fiction. He claims that Kafka strove to capture the complex nature of man's relation to God.

Anderson, Mark M. *Kafka's Clothes: Ornament and Aestheticism in the Habsburg* Fin de Siècle. Oxford: Clarendon Press, 1992.

In this critical volume, Mark Anderson focuses on the literary value of analyzing the ornaments and articles of clothing referenced in many of Kafka's fictions, including "The Metamorphosis." Other broad themes found in this book include decadence, aestheticism, the "physiognomy of guilt," culture, politics and many others.

Ben-Ephraim, Gavriel. "Making and breaking meaning: deconstruction, four-level allegory and 'The Metamorphosis.'" In *The Midwest Quarterly* 35.n4 (Summer 1994): 450–468.

In this essay, Ben-Ephraim discusses the allegory of the dung beetle in Franz Kafka's "The Metamorphosis," suggesting that its metaphysical nature proves problematic in the effort to deconstruct the work.

Boa, Elizabeth. *Kafka: Gender, Class, and Race in the Letters and Fictions*. Oxford: Clarendon Press, 1996.

In this critical volume, Elizabeth Boa addresses modernity, feminism, race, law and many other significant themes of literary discourse in the effort to analyze the rich, complex nature of Kafka's writing. In addition to "The Metamorphosis" and other select works of short fiction, Boa focuses on Kafka's letters to Felice Bauer and Milena Jesenská, as well as the unfinished novels *The Trial* and *The Castle*.

Brod, Max. *Franz Kafka: A Biography*. New York: Schocken Books, 1947.

Although this biography has a nostalgic slant to it, its perspective and importance are enhanced by the fact that Brod was Kafka's closest and most loyal friend. Many of Kafka's letters and unfinished manuscripts were left to Brod following Kafka's death.

Carrouges, Michel. Trans. By Emmett Parker. *Kafka Versus Kafka*. Tuscaloosa: University of Alabama Press, 1968.

This intensive study focuses on many aspects of Kafka's life and works. It includes chapters on Kafka's relationships with his father and fiancée, as well as his sickness, internal struggles, geopolitical conflicts, and faith.

Corngold, Stanley. *Franz Kafka: The Necessity of Form*. Ithaca: Cornell University Press, 1988.

In this critical volume, Stanley Corngold, a prominent Kafka scholar, provides extensive analysis on Kafka's career, the literary context within which he wrote, as well as his particular method of writing. Corngold focuses on Kafka's influences, his critical reception, and important considerations when engaging in serious Kafka study.

Flores, Angel. ed. *The Kafka Debate : New Perspectives for Our Time*. Staten Island: Gordian Press, 1977.

This critical volume, edited by Angel Flores, contains several original and reprinted essays from a wide range of Kafka scholars. The contents focus on such provocative themes as Narcissism, radicalism, Marxism, rhetoric, and much more.

Gans, Jerome S. "Narrative lessons for the psychotherapist: Kafka's "The Metamorphosis." In *American Journal of Psychotherapy* 52.n3 (Summer 1998): 352–367.

In this essay, Jerome Gans makes the case for what psychotherapists can gain from reading fiction, particularly Kafka's "The Metamorphosis." His essay uses "The Metamorphosis" as an example of how the therapist's interaction with fiction can inform his/her experience with a patient.

Harman, Mark. "Joyce and Kafka." In *The Sewanee Review* 101.n1 (Winter 1993): 66–85.

Harman's essay discusses the relationship between Irish and Jewish literary history, making the connection between the work and influences of Franz Kafka and the work and influences of James Joyce.

Hughes, Kenneth, ed. *Franz Kafka : an Anthology of Marxist Criticism*. Hanover: Clark University Press, 1981.

This critical anthology contains essays from a variety of international Kafka scholars, each interpreting and discussing Kafka's life and work through a Marxist lens. Kenneth Hughes is not only the editor of this volume, but he has also translated many of the works contained within.

Pawel, Ernest. *The Nightmare of Reason: A Life of Franz Kafka*. New York: Vintage Books, 1985.

In this text, Ernest Pawel offers a comprehensive study of Franz Kafka's life and influences, refraining from any heavy-handed analysis of Kafka's literary works.

Robertson, Ritchie. *Kafka: Judaism, Literature and Politics*. Oxford: Oxford University Press, 1987.

Robertson traces what he considers to be the most significant influences on Kafka's fiction. He focuses on

Kafka's German Jewish background; the writers and philosophers whose work had an impact on Kafka's fiction and the reception of his fiction; and the social and political circumstances in Europe during the early twentieth century.

Sokel, Walter H. "Kafka as a Jew." In *New Literary History* 30.4 (Autumn 1999): 837–854.

In this essay, Walter Sokel, a prominent Kafka scholar, provides an analysis of Kafka's literary technique, concentrating on Jewish influences. He provides background on the Jewish community in Prague, and influences from Yiddish theater and German Jewish culture, all with a keen eye on "The Metamorphosis."

Sokel, Walter H. *The Myth of Power and the Self: Essays on Franz Kafka.* Detroit: Wayne State University Press, 2002.

This current critical volume, from one of the foremost Kafka scholars, contains numerous essays on Kafka's life and work. It also has a comprehensive bibliography and index.

Stren, J.P., ed. *The World of Franz Kafka.* New York: Holt, Rinheart and Winston, 1980.

This volume contains a number of essays by Kafka scholars, focusing on varied angles of Kafka's life and work. It also contains over thirty illustrations of Kafka, his family, and Prague.

Thiher, Allen. *Franz Kafka: A Study of the Short Fiction.* Boston: Twayne Publishers, 1990.

Allen Thiher's volume provides an in depth study of Kafka's short fiction. In addition to literary analysis, Thiher also addresses some of Kafka's autobiographical writing, and provides a few extracts from contemporary Kafka scholarship.

Contributors

Harold Bloom is Sterling Professor of the Humanities at Yale University. He is the author of 30 books, including *Shelley's Mythmaking* (1959), *The Visionary Company* (1961), *Blake's Apocalypse* (1963), *Yeats* (1970), *A Map of Misreading* (1975), *Kabbalah and Criticism* (1975), *Agon: Toward a Theory of Revisionism* (1982), *The American Religion* (1992), *The Western Canon* (1994), and *Omens of Millennium: The Gnosis of Angels, Dreams, and Resurrection* (1996). *The Anxiety of Influence* (1973) sets forth Professor Bloom's provocative theory of the literary relationships between the great writers and their predecessors. His most recent books include *Shakespeare: The Invention of the Human* (1998), a 1998 National Book Award finalist, *How to Read and Why* (2000), *Genius: A Mosaic of One Hundred Exemplary Creative Minds* (2002), *Hamlet: Poem Unlimited* (2003), *Where Shall Wisdom Be Found?* (2004), and *Jesus and Yahweh: The Names Divine* (2005). In 1999, Professor Bloom received the prestigious American Academy of Arts and Letters Gold Medal for Criticism. He has also received the International Prize of Catalonia, the Alfonso Reyes Prize of Mexico, and the Hans Christian Andersen Bicentennial Prize of Denmark.

Aaron Tillman is a lecturer in the division of Arts and Humanities at Babson College. His fiction has appeared in *Glimmer Train*.

Mark M. Anderson has taught in the German department at Columbia University. He has published several books including *The Broken Boat* and *In the Storm of Roses: Selected Poems by Ingeborg Bachmann*.

Stanley Corngold has been a professor of German and Comparative Literature at Princeton University. He is one of the preeminent Kafka scholars, author of *The Commentators'*

Despair: The Interpretation of Kafka's Metamorphosis, and editor of an annotated critical edition of *The Metamprphosis.*

George Gibian has taught at Smith College. His publications include the essay "Dichtung und Wahrheit: Three Versions of Reality in Franz Kafka" which was published in *The German Quarterly.*

M. Elizabeth Macandrew has taught at Columbia University and has written about Richardson and Fielding. Her publications include the essay "A Splacknuck and a Dung-Beetle: Realism and Probability in Swift and Kafka" which was published in *College English.*

Philip H. Rhein has taught at Vanderbilt University. His publications include the book *The Urge to Live: A Comparative Study of Franz Kafka's Der Prozess and Albert Camus' L'etranger* and the essay "Two Fantastic Visions: Franz Kafka and Alfred Kubin" which was published in the *South Atlantic Bulletin.*

Michael Rowe has been a clinical professor of sociology at Yale. His publications have crossed genres, including an essay on Franz Kafka, "*Metamorphosis:* Defending the Human," which was published in *Literature and Medicine.*

Michael P. Ryan has written several articles on literature and Eastern Philosophy, including "Kafka's *Die Söhne*: The Range and Scope of Metaphor" and "Samsa and *Samsara*: Suffering, Death, and Rebirth in 'The Metamorphosis'" which was published in the *German Quarterly.*

Mark Spilka has taught at the University of Michigan. His publications include the book *Dickens and Kafka: A Mutual Interpretation* and the essay "Kafka's Sources for 'The Metamorphosis'" which was published in *Comparative Literature.*

Peter Stine has taught at Wayne State University. His publications include the essay "Franz Kafka and Animals" which was published in *Contemporary Literature*.

Allen Thiher has been a professor of French at the University of Missouri. He has written articles on modern literature, philosophy and film. His books include *Céline, The Novel as Delerium, The Cinematic Muse* and *Words in Reflection: Modern Language Theory and Postmodern Fiction*.

Acknowledgments

Anderson, Mark M. "Sliding Down the Evolutionary Ladder?: Aesthetic Autonomy in *The Metamorphosis.*" In *Kafka's Clothes: Ornament and Aestheticism in the Habsburg* Fin de Siècle. Oxford: Clarendon Press, 1992, pp. 125–126. © 1992 Mark M. Anderson. Reprinted by permission of Oxford University Press.

Corngold, Stanley. "*The Metamorphosis:* Metamorphosis of the Metaphor." In *Franz Kafka: The Necessity of Form.* Ithaca: Cornell University Press, 1988, pp. 57–58. © 1988 by Cornell University Press. Reprinted by permission.

Gibeon, George. "Dichtung und Wahrheit: Three Versions of Reality in Franz Kafka." In *The German Quarterly*, Vol. 30, No.1 (Jan., 1957), pp. 29–31. © 1957 by the American Association of Teachers of German. Reprinted by permission.

Macandrew, M. Elizabeth. "A Splacknuck and a Dung-Beetle: Realism and Probability in Swiftand Kafka." In *College English*, Vol. 31, No.4 (Jan., 1970), pp. 387–389. © 1970 by the National Council of Teachers of English. Reprinted by permission.

Rhein, Philip H. "Two Fantastic Visions: Franz Kafka and Alfred Kubin." In *South Atlantic Bulletin*, Vol. 42, No. 2 (May, 1977), pp. 62–64. © 1977 by South Atlantic Modern Language Association. Reprinted by permission.

Rowe, Michael. "*Metamorphosis:* Defending the Human." In *Literature and Medicine*, Vol. 21, No.2 (Fall 2002), pp. 267–268. © 2002 by The Johns Hopkins University Press. Reprinted by permission.

Ryan, Michael P. "Samsa and *Samsara*: Suffering, Death, and Rebirth in 'The Metamorphosis.'" In *German Quarterly*, 72.2

(Spring 1999), pp. 136–137. © 1999 by the American Association of Teachers of German. Reprinted by permission.

Spilka, Mark. "Kafka's Sources for 'The Metamorphosis.'" In *Comparative Literature*, Vol. 11, No. 4 (Autumn, 1959), pp. 290–292. © 1959 by the University of Oregon. Reprinted by permission.

Stine, Peter. "Franz Kafka and Animals." In *Contemporary Literature*, Vol. 22, No.1 (Winter, 1981), pp. 62–64. © 1981 by the University of Wisconsin Press. Reprinted by permission.

Thiher, Allen. "'The Judgment' and 'The Metamorphosis.'" In *Franz Kafka: A Study of the Short Fiction*. Boston: Twayne Publishers, 1990, pp. 48–50. © 1990 by the Gale Group, Inc. Reprinted by permission of the Gale Group, Inc.

Every effort has been made to contact the owners of copyrighted material and secure copyright permission. Articles appearing in this volume generally appear much as they did in their original publication with few or no editorial changes. Those interested in locating the original source will find bibliographic information in the bibliography and acknowledgments sections of this volume.

Index

PT
2621
.A26
V4282